Liverpool and it

Mike Clarke

Acknowledgements

Many people have helped with the research for this book, there really are too many to list. Amongst the more important are Adrian Jarvis, now retired from Merseyside Maritime Museums, who asked me to write the first edition and helped with suggestions for sources. The staff at Liverpool Record Office and the Maritime Record Centre have both been of great help in sorting out material, as have staff at British Waterways, especially Tom Rayward at Leeds. The Liverpool staff of the Waterways Regeneration Task Force, especially Richard Longton, who are planning and constructing the new canal link across Pier Head were also able to offer information and provide illustrations. Also thanks to the staff at Landmark for publishing what I hope is an informative book.

Landmark Publishing

Published by

Ashbourne Hall, Cokayne Ave
Ashbourne, Derbyshire, DE6 1EJ England
Tel: (01335) 347349 Fax: (01335) 347303
e-mail: landmark@clara.net

2nd Edition

13 ISBN: 978-1-84306-336-0

10 ISBN: 1-84306-336-0

British Library Cataloguing in Publication Data: a catalogue record for this book is available from the British Library.

Print: Cromwell Press

Design by: Michelle Hunt

Edited by: Ian Howe

Front Cover: Parkes' *Bembo* passing under the new Coffee House Bridge in the 1930s

Back Cover Main: Canal Boats in Salthouse Dock for the Mersey River Festival

Back Cover Bottom Right: Stanley Dock and the canal branch to the river

Back cover Bottom Middle: Skinny-dipping at Burlington Street Bridge in the mid-1890s

Back cover Bottom Left: Liverpool terminus

Page 3: Bootle

Photo Credits

Merseyside Maritime Museum, p16, 79; Liverpool Record Office, p21, 23 bottom, 26 middle, 29, 30, 32, 45 top, 51 bottom, 52, 53 top, 55 top, 57 bottom, 59, 79 bottom; British Waterways, p81 top, 83 & 84; Boat Museum Archive, 39 bottom; Jack Parkinson, p26, 41, 58 bottom; Daily Post and Echo, p55 bottom, p74; Roy Gibbons, 56 top

Liverpool and its Canal

Mike Clarke

Landmark Publishing

Contents

INTRODUCTION

From the start of the eighteenth century, local canals and river navigations linked to the Mersey have had a major effect on Liverpool. Not only did canal boats bring mundane articles, like coal, but also sumptuous ones such as fine porcelain from the kilns of the Potteries and rich textiles from the looms of East Lancashire. Canal barges from Wigan, Blackburn, Runcorn, Ellesmere Port and elsewhere on local inland waterways mingled in the docks with shipping from around the world. It was a bustling panorama, which changed rapidly as boats were loaded and unloaded. Cargoes were carried to and from warehouses on the docks or those alongside the Leeds & Liverpool Canal. The architecture of the docks and warehouses matched the quality of the goods passing through them. Jesse Hartley, Liverpool's Dock Engineer in the second half of the nineteenth century, was the architect for many of these 'cathedrals' of the Industrial Revolution, putting Liverpool at the forefront of building design and construction.

When the Leeds & Liverpool Canal was first opened in 1774, its terminus was on the northern outskirts of Liverpool. The canal passed through open countryside before reaching the village of Bootle. However, industry was attracted to the banks of the canal by the cheap and easy supply of coal from Wigan, and houses for workers were erected at many places along the canal. Pollution from industry was to drive the wealthy from their homes in Everton, and some settled in the suburbs beyond Litherland, where canal passenger boats provided them with a commuter service into Liverpool.

As the docks were extended northwards, more industries were established on the canalside, and this commercial growth increased when the branch canal was built down to Stanley Dock in the 1840s. It was not just manufacturing industry which was attracted by the canal; service industries also developed alongside the canal's banks. The local gas industry relied upon the ca-

nal, as did the town's manure and refuse department in the days before mains sewers. All in all, the canal had a major effect on the development of the town, providing not just transport facilities for commerce and the docks, but also leisure potential for the public, a service it is increasingly providing today.

Times change, and shipping has become concentrated in the northern docks where modern methods ensure the speedy turnaround demanded today. The southern docks closed, with several being filled in, and the same fate almost overcame the Leeds & Liverpool Canal. But the regeneration benefits of waterfront sites were recognised in time, and now the south docks and the canal have a new role to play in Liverpool's cultural and social life.

But boats are needed to give life to water space. Just as barges, brightly decorated with traditional designs, animated the docks when they were used for handling cargoes, so today pleasure boats can bring life to the open waters of the southern docks. There is a problem; since the Liver Building was built on the site of the old George's Dock in 1906, there has not been an easy and safe way for canal boats to reach the south docks from the Leeds & Liverpool Canal at Stanley Dock.

To address this problem, and bring vitality back to the south docks, British Waterways has developed a scheme to link the north and south docks across Pier Head. After extensive consultation with the local community, the plan is to build a new canal in front of the Liver Building. The canal link will bring the benefits of canal restoration to Liverpool, making the city a key destination on the national inland waterway network.

This book will help to explain the importance of canals to Liverpool's history, and provide a guide to the industrial and social heritage of the Leeds & Liverpool Canal on Merseyside. It was first published in 1992, and has been enlarged and updated.

1. THE EARLY YEARS

At the start of the eighteenth century, Liverpool was about to evolve from a minor harbour serving the Irish trade into a major international port. Many factors led to the development of the town as England's premier port: its geographical location on the west coast, ideally suited for trade with the increasingly important colonial markets in America and Africa; the entrepreneurial skills of its merchants; and, less well known, the arrival of the engineer Thomas Steers in 1710 to construct the town's first dock. Steers was not just Liverpool's first Dock Engineer, but was also to become involved in the political and economic life of the town. For centuries ships had been loaded and unloaded whilst moored in the tidal river. The dock which he built, the first commercial wet dock in the country, allowed greater security for cargoes, with less interference from the weather and tides during transshipment. It was also an important shipbuilding and repairing facility. However, it was Steers' realisation of the importance of transport links with the town's hinterland, and his active development of them, which was to provide the real foundation for Liverpool's success.

Less than three years after Steers' arrival in the town he had produced two surveys for river navigations: one up the Douglas to Wigan, the other up the Mersey and Irwell to Manchester. In these plans his was ahead of his time as they were not completed until 1742 and 1736 respectively. Inland navigations were expensive to promote and build, and people were still unsure about their benefits. Despite early setbacks, he maintained an interest in inland transport, and by the time of his death in 1750 he had surveyed the Calder & Hebble Navigation in Yorkshire and the Boyne Navigation in Ireland, had completed Britain's first summit level canal, the Newry Canal, also in Ireland, and was involved with the turnpike road from Liverpool to Prescot. Under Steers' influence, Liverpool's Town Council realised the importance of inland transport and Steers' apprentice and successor, Henry Berry, was allowed time off from his duties as Dock

Map showing the major works of Thomas Steers.

Engineer to build the Sankey Navigation, opened in 1757, from the Mersey at Warrington to the St Helens coalfield. Although built under a river navigation Act, it was an entirely still-water canal, and marks an important step in the development of Britain's inland waterways. Earlier, the Council had been involved with the Weaver Navigation and, following the success of the Duke of Bridgewater's Canal from Worsley to Manchester, granted money towards the cost of surveying two proposed canals, the Grand Trunk (Trent & Mersey Canal) and the Leeds & Liverpool Canal. There were other canal proposals associated with the town, which are discussed later.

The Douglas Navigation

Perhaps the main forerunner of the Leeds & Liverpool Canal in Lancashire was the Douglas Navigation, whose main purpose was to open up the Wigan coalfield and to provide Liverpool with a secure supply of coal. In the early eighteenth century, most of the town's coal came by road from Prescot, a route which was almost impassable during winter weather. There were coalfields on the Dee and in Cumbria, but they were more involved with the Dublin market, and Liverpool was struggling to find a regular supply. Thomas Steers made his first survey of the navigation in 1713, but failed to get an Act of Parliament in that year. He tried again in 1720, this time successfully, his partner being William Squire, son of a well-established local family. Squire went down to London to raise the finance, but became involved with the South Sea Bubble, a time of financial manipulation and mismanagement. The Douglas was one of the few sound companies being promoted, and its shares soon rose from £5 to £70 — they fell even quicker. Unfortunately Squire became involved in the bubble, and though he sent some money up to Steers, most was lost. Squire does not seem to have returned to Liverpool, and the last we hear of him is a message to customs officials asking for his detention as he had been defrauding a London charity. Steers did begin construction of the navigation, building one lock and starting a second, and straightening and deepening part of the river near Rufford, but he soon ran out of money.

Work began again in the mid-1730s, after the scheme had been taken over by Alexander Leigh, a Wigan attorney and agent for the Earl of Balcarres, who lived at Haigh Hall and had extensive coal mining interests. Steers was still involved, being called in from time to time to advise on aspects of construction. The navigation opened in 1741, allowing boats to trade between the Wigan coalfield and the Ribble estuary. By 1770 it was carrying about 15,000 tons of coal annually, some destined for the Irish market, though many ports on the Lancashire coast, including Liverpool, were also served. Coal was usually transshipped from the smaller river boats into larger coastal vessels at Sollom or Tarleton. Other goods carried included ashes and kelp for soap manufacture, potatoes, grain and limestone, one of the most important mid-eighteenth-century cargoes. The coal and cannel brought by the navigation from the Douglas Valley were of high quality and sold for higher prices than coal from elsewhere. Cannel burnt with a bright flame, leaving little ash, which made it very suitable for household use. Later it became the main fuel used in Liverpool to produce gas when works were established in the town in 1815.

A lock on the Newry Canal. Opened in the 1740s, it was the first summit level canal in Britain, and the first canal to use ground paddles, where the sluices for filling the lock are built into the lock walls. This enabled deeper locks to be built and was first used in Britain on the Newry Canal by Steers.

Little survives of the Douglas Navigation today. This weir at Dean Lock, near Wigan, was built in 1740 and is the only structure remaining from the original navigation. It can be seen from the towpath.

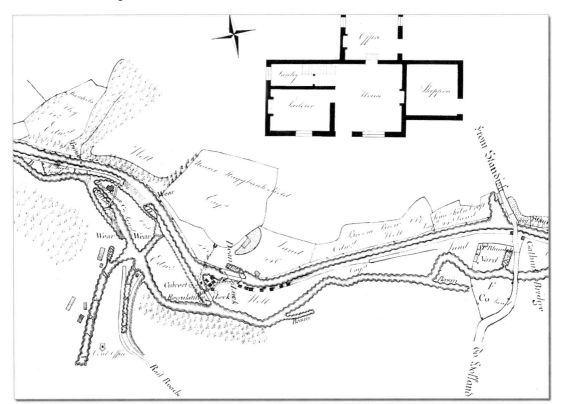

The area had several coal wharfs as can be seen from the map of 1802.

Just a hole in a field at Douglas Chapel, Parbold, on a bend in the river.

The success of navigations, such as the Douglas, Weaver and Mersey & Irwell laid the foundation for Britain's canal revolution. When the Duke of Bridgewater came to build his canal in the 1760s, he would probably have been less enthusiastic if he had not seen the potential in the already established north-west navigations.

Promoting the Leeds & Liverpool Canal

The proposal for a canal linking Leeds with the Irish Sea had first been raised in the *York Courant* on 7th August 1764. Initially it was the merchants and coal-owners of Bradford, headed by John Stanhope, who took up the suggestion. They were anxious to increase Bradford's supply of lime from Craven. It was used as a fertiliser for the improvement of land, and for mortar and decoration in building work, whilst limestone was used for purifying iron smelted in ironworks around Bradford. Lime was obtained by burning limestone from Craven with coal from local mines, mainly those around Stockbridge at this time.

An earlier unsuccessful plan to make the River Aire navigable to Skipton, in 1743, was proposed for the same reason. Besides this local traffic in lime, they hoped that a canal to Liverpool would enable them to increase and cheapen imports from Ireland and the colonies, and export locally produced woollen goods to the expanding international markets. The Yorkshire men called a meeting in Bradford in 1766 to promote the scheme and over one hundred subscribers paid towards the cost of making a plan and estimate. This was undertaken by John Longbotham who presented his initial survey to the promoters at a meeting in Bradford on 7th January 1768. At this meeting it was suggested that the canal should also be promoted in, and subscriptions obtained from, Lancashire.

The merchants in Yorkshire, who had long been exporting woollen goods to Europe, were well established with secure finances. Many were Quakers with links to Quaker bankers in Settle and East Anglia, and this enabled them to organise the promotion and financing of the canal relatively easily. In Lancashire, industry was only just beginning to develop beyond the production of goods for the local market, and money was scarce. It was mainly in Liverpool, where the colonial trades were rapidly increasing, and in

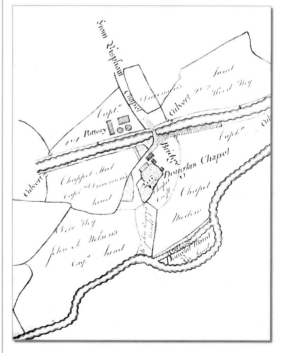

The 1802 map shows that it may hide the remains of a Douglas Navigation lock.

9

A view of Liverpool around 1800 showing some of the many windmills which used to serve the town.

Colne, already heavily involved in the woollen trades, that merchants and local gentry were able to see the benefit of such a project and have the necessary finance. Despite interest in the canal not being so forthcoming elsewhere in Lancashire, the Corporation of Liverpool took the initiative by suggesting that James Brindley should check Longbotham's survey for the scheme. They had already given £200 towards the cost of Longbotham's survey and now offered a further £50 towards that of Brindley. Interest in the canal was slower to develop elsewhere in Lancashire, but a meeting was eventually held at Preston on 25th August 1768 when a Lancashire committee of forty was nominated.

A joint meeting of the two committees was held in Burnley in December 1768 when it was agreed to apply to Parliament for the necessary powers to build the canal. It was too late for the 1769 session so there was a year's wait during which some of the Liverpool promoters became unhappy about the route, proposing a different line through Wigan. Their motive was coal.

A Compromise over the Route

The Yorkshire promoters wanted the canal for two reasons: to improve the supply of lime and limestone from Craven to the Bradford district, and for carrying imported wool and other commodities from Liverpool or Hull, and woollen goods for export through Liverpool. To achieve this their line went up the Aire valley from a junction with the Aire & Calder Navigation in Leeds, through the Craven limestone district, from there to Padiham, the Ribble Valley and then through Parbold directly to Liverpool. This plan was opposed by the Liverpool promoters who required a canal which would give them a regular and cheap supply of coal. Throughout the eighteenth century Liverpool was Lancashire's most important industrial centre, where pottery, chemicals, sugar, salt, copper and many other products were manufactured or refined. It was only when land prices and wages became significantly higher than in neighbouring areas of Lancashire, and when problems with pollution for the affluent merchants increased dramatically, that the town ceased being a major industrial centre. The Sankey Navigation and its proprietors had been supplying these industries with coal since 1757, and their virtual monopoly allowed them to raise prices. By providing a second source of coal for the town, the Liverpool merchants hoped that the Leeds & Liverpool Canal would reduce the price and increase the availability of coal. To do this the canal had to pass through a suitable coalfield, so the Liverpool promoters produced a scheme for the canal which passed through the Douglas Valley to the coalfields of Wigan and Chorley, Yorkshire being reached via Blackburn and Burnley. At the same time there was some discussion about whether the canal should be for narrow boats or wide boats. Brindley, under whose guidance the Grand Trunk (Trent & Mersey Canal) had changed from a wide to a narrow canal, was to assess the two routes, and some pressure was exerted on him to ensure that the canal was a wide one.

The conflict over the route was hard-fought, but through the arbitration of John Hustler of Bradford a compromise was arranged. The canal would be built from both ends simultaneously, which allowed both groups to achieve their main aims quickly; limestone would be available from Craven for Bradford and coal could be brought from Wigan, via the Douglas Navigation, to Parbold and the canal to Liverpool. At this time, the main line of the canal was still to pass

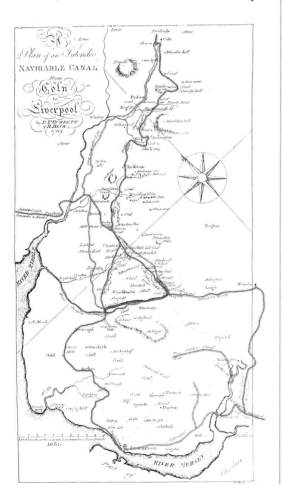

through the Ribble Valley and the sparsely populated area to the north of Blackburn. It was not until 1793, with the East Lancashire textile industry increasing in importance, that the route through Burnley and Blackburn to Wigan was substituted. Even then, the section from Wheelton (near Chorley) to Aspull (near Wigan) was never built, the Lancaster Canal being used instead.

Other Liverpool Canal Proposals

At this time, the Wigan coalfield was seen as the solution to all Liverpool's coal supply problems. Since 1757, the Sankey Navigation had allowed coal from the southern section of this coalfield to reach Liverpool, but boats had to sail down the tidal estuary to Liverpool, which could be difficult in winter or at neap tides. Up until 1774, when the Leeds & Liverpool opened, the navigation had a virtual monopoly of the coal trade which kept prices high. To provide competition, other canals, besides the Leeds & Liverpool, were proposed. The first, in 1769, may have started as a branch from the Leeds & Liverpool Canal to join with the Sankey and the Wigan coalfield. This would have created a still-water link with the coalfield, avoiding the need to use the estuary. It was to run from the centre of Liverpool to Widnes, where it would cross the Mersey on an aqueduct to join the Bridgewater Canal. A branch from near Hale would head towards St Helens and the coalfield there. The aqueduct over the Mersey was probably too ambitious for the time, and a second, simpler, scheme was proposed in 1771. This was to pass eastwards through Walton and Huyton before turning northwards towards Wigan at Farnworth. The Sankey Navigation would be crossed at Newton-le-Willows, and at Wigan there would be connections with the Douglas Navigation and the Lancaster Canal's original route connect-

Left: The 1769 Burdett map of the various canal routes proposed and built in Lancashire. The Leeds & Liverpool Canal was originally to follow the Ribble Valley to Whalley, with the Liverpool proprietors' proposed route through Blackburn and Burnley also being shown. The first proposal for the Lancaster Canal is shown, forming a link to the Bridgewater Canal at Leigh. The proposed canal from Liverpool to coal mines near Prescot and to Runcorn is also shown.

ing Chorley with Leigh and the Bridgewater Canal. A Bill was presented to Parliament in 1772 and again the following year, but the lack of support from local landowners resulted in its failure. The people behind both schemes were, in the main, those who had promoted the variation in the Leeds & Liverpool's line in 1769. Obviously, some were still upset that their route was not taken up, and they did not think that the line authorised would supply sufficient coal. It was the purchase of the Douglas Navigation by the Leeds & Liverpool in 1772 which overcame these objections, and possibly led to the Liverpool Canal Bill's failure. The idea of a second canal from Liverpool was raised again in 1793 in an effort to lower tolls on coal on the Leeds & Liverpool Canal. A canal to Manchester was suggested, passing through Winstanley, Bickerstaffe

and Rainford, but once again came to nothing.

Later, in 1825, the engineer Francis Giles produced a scheme for a canal close to the Mersey as part of a plan for improved road and canal links to London. Both the new road and canal would have crossed the Mersey on an aqueduct at Runcorn. In Cheshire, the canal would join the Bridgewater Canal and, in Lancashire, the extension of the Sankey Navigation in Widnes. However, growing interest in the Liverpool & Manchester Railway probably ensured the idea remained dormant.

The Canal Opens

After agreement over the choice of route through East Lancashire had been reached by the Lancashire and

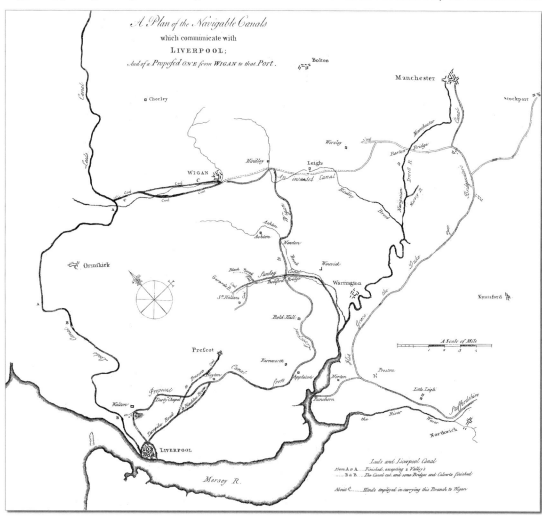

A map of the proposed Liverpool Canal of 1772 which was to cross the Sankey Navigation near St Helens on its way to the Douglas Navigation in Wigan

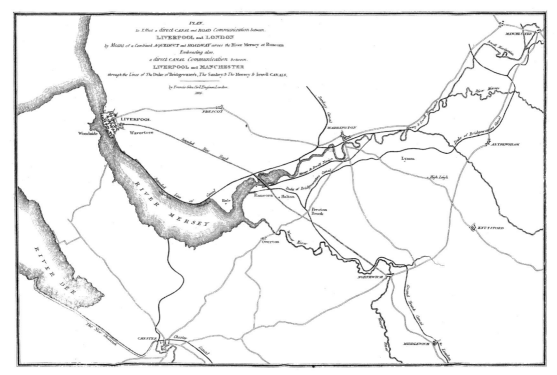

The 1825 canal proposed from Liverpool to Runcorn with its associated road.

Yorkshire promoters, they presented their Bill for the Leeds & Liverpool Canal to Parliament. An Act was quickly obtained and construction commenced on 5th November 1770 on the deep cutting at Halsall, one of the largest excavation works on the canal.

Initially Alexander Leigh, majority owner of the Douglas Navigation, had opposed the Leeds & Liverpool Canal scheme as he was worried that the aqueduct over the navigation at Parbold would restrict the size of boat capable of using his navigation, and prevent the passage of sailing vessels with fixed masts. He was already in the process of removing fixed bridges and replacing them with swing bridges for this purpose. Clauses were inserted in the canal's Act to protect the navigation by requiring a flight of locks from the river to the canal at Parbold and a branch from there to the Navigation at Dean, near Gathurst. On early canal maps, before 1771, it was marked as Leigh's cut. As designed, the branch was intended to have swing bridges so that sailing boats could reach Wigan, but in 1771 Leigh agreed to the sale of the Navigation to the canal company, and the branch was built by them with stone overbridges. Sailing barges may not have been able to use it, but the branch allowed Liverpool to be supplied with coal from the Wigan area. There was one lock, at Appley Bridge,

which was built large enough to allow boats 70 feet long by 14 feet 6 inches wide to pass, large enough for boats similar to small local coasting vessels to use the canal between Wigan and Liverpool.

Unfortunately the estimated cost for the canal was found to be extremely optimistic. The company was only able to afford to build the sections from Leeds to Holme Bridge Lock, Gargrave, which opened by 1777, and from Liverpool to Parbold, with the branch to the Douglas Navigation at Dean, opened in 1774, before running out of money. However, as these sections allowed limestone to reach Bradford, and coal to reach Liverpool, neither group of proprietors was unduly worried. The American War of Independence made raising money for further construction difficult, and it was not until 1790 that they again began to think once more about connecting the two halves of the canal.

The only additional work undertaken before then was the elimination of the old Douglas Navigation which had fallen into a very dilapidated state. The way this was done shows that there were still considerable differences between the Lancashire and Yorkshire committees. Work was started by the Lancashire men on the section from Dean to Wigan, with their

Richard, of coal carriers Richard Williams, was a typical square-sterned horse-drawn boat as used on the Leeds & Liverpool Canal. Note the fine decoration which was found on many Leeds & Liverpool Canal boats in Lancashire.

Steam power was used from the 1880s, with *William Robinson*, seen here at Bingley, being typical.

maintenance engineer, Robert Dickenson, in charge. The locks on this length were built for boats 70 feet in length, the same size at that at Appley Bridge as boats had already been built to these dimensions. The canal from Burscough to Rufford, however, was built by the Yorkshire committee's engineer Richard Owen, with locks of the same size as those in Yorkshire, 62 feet long by 14 feet 6 inches wide. It seems amazing that such a situation should occur, the only explanation being the stubbornness of the Yorkshire men who had a controlling interest in the canal. Their attitude continued into the nineteenth century. When the Leigh Branch was built in 1819 the locks were of the shorter Yorkshire size, despite linking with the Bridgewater Canal which took 70-foot-long boats. It was only after Pickfords complained in 1820, six months after the branch had opened, that their narrow boats could not reach Liverpool that the locks from Leigh to Wigan were lengthened to match those from Wigan to Liverpool. From Wigan into Yorkshire the locks can only take boats of 62 feet in length.

The Boats

The Sankey Navigation, opened in 1757, was built to take boats 68 feet long by 16 feet six inches wide, which allowed a typical Irish Sea trading vessel to pass. Locks on the Douglas were narrower and could only be used by smaller coastal and river craft. On the Leeds & Liverpool Canal in Lancashire, the locks were built 14 feet 6 inches wide to suit the smaller type of boat. Thus they were long enough to accommodate narrow boats, which were only 7 feet wide and 68 feet long (later up to 72 feet long). They had been developed on the Bridgewater Canal and were used on canals in the Midlands. Such boats were easy to build and some had been used on the construction of the Lancashire section of the Leeds & Liverpool Canal. They were subsequently sold for use by traders on the canal and could carry from 15 to 18 tons. It seems likely that these boats were only used while traffic was being developed and that as trade increased new wide boats were built to suit the locks. Many of these had square sterns, similar to the flats working on the Mersey, and could carry about 35 tons (by the mid-twentieth century, boats on the canal carried 50 tons). To increase the speed at which boats passed through locks the round stern was used, as this enabled the boatman to start shutting the lock gates before the boat was fully into the lock.

Boats on the Douglas Navigation had been hauled by men, but when the Leeds & Liverpool Canal was built a towpath was provided which enabled horses to be used. Sailing boats delivered coal from Wigan to Liverpool after the Leigh Branch joined the Bridgewater Canal in 1820. They were horse-drawn along the canals, and only sailed down the Mersey estuary. It was only after a link was built from the main canal to Stanley Dock, in 1846, that sailing flats appeared on the canal in Liverpool. Even then their masts were lowered and they were also towed by horse to their destination. Usually dumb boats (without sails or engine) were used, as they could pass more easily through Great Howard Street bridge at the entrance to the branch canal. Steam-driven tugs were tried in the 1850s on the Wigan coal traffic, but it was not until the 1880s that steam was used regularly, especially for merchandise boats. Single and twin-cylinder diesel engines began to be fitted in the 1920s, and eventually became the usual method of propulsion.

There were two main types of canal boat: those for carrying minerals and manure, and those for grain and merchandise. The holds of the former were left open to the weather, while to keep the holds of the latter dry, sheets and coamings were provided. Living accommodation for the boatmen and their families was provided in cabins at the bow and stern. Although some families did live on board, the majority had a house ashore. Many boatmen came from the West Lancashire canalside villages, particularly Burscough. A few came from the Liverpool area, the majority living in houses near the Bootle canal depot.

The Canal and Liverpool's Development

Following the opening of the canal in 1774 trade increased rapidly. Many canal proprietors, from both Liverpool and Yorkshire, invested in the Douglas Valley coal mines, their money enabling these mines to be enlarged. Some 15,000 tons of coal had been sent down the Douglas to Tarleton in the years prior to the opening of the canal. This traffic increased slightly after the canal opened, but was soon marginalised by the tonnages sent to Liverpool. In 1780 almost 36,000 tons were delivered, and this had increased to over 137,000 tons ten years later, more than ten times the tonnage of merchandise carried. Industry, which had previously been located near the docks, was soon attracted to the canal by this plentiful supply of coal, with chemical, glass and brickworks being

Stanley Dock and the canal branch to the river were built in the1840s. This photo taken during the Second World War shows the variety of boats and barges which used the dock and the canal in Liverpool. Note Jesse Hartley's imposing warehouses, similar to those he built at Albert Dock.

erected on its banks. The canal also provided a safe and smooth passage for people, the first packet boat between Liverpool and Wigan operating from May 1776 at a charge of 1d. per mile per person.

The terminal basin at Old Hall Street was regularly enlarged to cope with increased traffic, but no other major work was undertaken on the Lancashire section of the canal in the eighteenth century apart from bypassing the Douglas Navigation. Sufficient money to begin completing the canal was eventually raised in the 1790s, with work restarting on the Yorkshire end. Progress was slow and finances precarious, with much of the canal's profit put towards the new works, to the detriment of dividends. There were further conflicts over the route, particularly with the Lancaster Canal, but a compromise was finally reached and a through route opened from Liverpool to Leeds in 1816. Four years later the Leigh branch was completed, linking the canal at Wigan with the Bridgewater Canal and forming a route from Liverpool to the Midlands and the south. The only outstanding part of the original scheme was a link to the river, and this was to take a further 26 years to complete.

Later Years

From 1816 the canal had a virtual monopoly on trade to East Lancashire and a dominant hold on Liverpool's coal supply. This was short-lived as fourteen years later the Liverpool & Manchester Railway opened. Trade with Wigan, Leigh and Manchester was affected, but it was not until the East Lancashire Railway entered Liverpool in 1848 that the canal's main traffics began to be challenged. After two years of severe competition an agreement was reached, in 1850, for merchandise traffic on the canal to be leased to a group of railway companies for 21 years. This gave the canal company a guaranteed income and though the railways siphoned off traffic, it enabled the canal to build up its reserves. These were then used to improve the canal's facilities when the lease was given up and enabled the canal to compete effectively with the railways in the latter part of the nineteenth century.

There had always been a considerable traffic with the docks, with goods carried to and from the canal basin by horse drawn lorries. A link into the docks would have overcome the inconvenience of trans-shipping, and this had been allowed in the canal's first Act. It was finally achieved in 1846, 76 years later, when a branch was built from the new Stanley Dock, enabling goods and coal to be interchanged without the use of road transport.

During the nineteenth century many of the manufacturing industries on the canal banks closed, though they were replaced by service industries, such as gasworks and warehousing, which resulted in a continual increase in the traffic carried during the century. However, tolls fell with railway competition and this adversely affected the dividend paid to the canal's shareholders. In an effort to improve matters following the surrender of the railway lease of merchandise traffic in 1873, considerable amounts of money were spent on new warehousing, particularly in Liverpool and Bootle. The company also built up their own fleet of boats for the carriage of merchandise and towards the end of the century were taking traffic away from the railways, especially the Lancashire & Yorkshire Railway.

Unfortunately their success was part of their downfall: people knew their finances were sound. There had been complaints from coal owners over compensation for coal left under the canal to stop subsidence. This was only done where there were locks, tunnels or aqueducts, but as mines became deeper, more coal had to be left, which interfered with colliery operation. Local authorities also complained over the canal's low rateable value, though this did not affect Liverpool. The canal had to pay a quarter of its rateable value under the Public Health Act of 1848, but in Liverpool they had to pay the full rate under Liverpool's 1846 Public Health Act. Things came to a head in 1891, when the canal had to obtain an Act for its new reservoir at Winterburn. Opposition was only overcome by substantial financial concessions from the company. The Railway & Canal Traffic Act of 1888, which limited tolls, also had the effect of reducing income to a canal. Money was already earmarked for the improvements to the canal it was making, such as building new warehouses and deepening the canal and improving the banks, particularly in Lancashire. There was also a scheme to lengthen the locks and increase the size of boats so that they could carry 100 tons, which dated back to the 1890s. The First World War also brought financial difficulties with canals treated less favourably, with respect to Government compensation, than railways. After this, all improvement schemes were abandoned.

In the 1920s and '30s the introduction of the lorry and the decline of traditional industries on whom the canal had relied were the precursor to the end of carrying. Large tonnages continued only because industries using coal continued to be supplied by canal. Tate & Lyle's and the gasworks at Linacre and Athol Street continued to be served into the 1960s. But the severe winter of 1963, when the canal was closed for several months, and the decline in the quality of coal from Wigan, making it unsuitable for the gas industry, brought an end to trade on the canal. There were attempts to restart traffic, notably the carriage of grain from the docks to Manchester around 1980, but by then the condition of the canal had deteriorated, making regular trade difficult.

2. THE TERMINAL BASIN

By the mid-1760s Liverpool was established as one of the country's major ports, with almost a thousand ships leaving every year. The Old Dock and the Salthouse Dock had already been built, with George's Dock and Duke's Dock soon to open. Industry was developing: the manufacture of pottery, soap, ironwork and glass-ware, and the processing of salt, copper and sugar were well established, while the importation of cotton was beginning, though few textile mills were ever erected in the town. Having direct links with the trade of the port, these industries tended to be along the river front, and consequently the wealthy were beginning to move out of the centre of the town to the less developed high ground to the east. It was into this rapidly changing scene that the Leeds & Liverpool proposed to enter.

Land was always cheapest away from town centres, which were consequently avoided during the construction of the Leeds & Liverpool. Subsequently, as industry developed because of the improved services it provided, towns expanded out to encompass the canal. This happened in Liverpool where the canal entered from the less developed north, though even here Lord Derby demanded higher prices for his land than elsewhere on the canal, an indication of the pace of expansion in the town rather than his avarice.

For the town's merchants the canal's main purpose was the supply of coal; not just for industrial and domestic use, but also for export, particularly to Ireland. The market for coal was enormous; in 1794, twenty years after the canal had opened, over 150,000 tons were being delivered annually, and several of the canal's proprietors had become coal merchants, with their mines located in the Douglas valley near Wigan. The effect on the town was immediate, with industry developing on land owned by the canal company between Vauxhall Road and Love Lane. Because of the improved services which the canal provided, land in this area was to rise in value, becoming too expensive for housing. Thus the canal came to dominate the development of the northern side of the town for many years. Its effects on land use can still be seen today, though with more difficulty as the canal corridor is redeveloped.

The Original Basin

At first the canal's terminal basin was on the edge of the town, at the end of Old Hall Street. Princes Dock was not to be built for almost fifty years and townsfolk took the air on 'Ladies Walk', an avenue lined with elm trees, which ran down to the river from Old Hall Street. Alongside the river were the seawater baths, erected in 1765, from which Bath Street took its name. These were used by the wealthy while ordinary folk used the beach to the north. Back on the canal there were coal wharfs on the east side of the basin, merchandise being handled on a wharf on Old Hall Street. A dry dock for repairing boats was available a few hundred yards from the end of the canal, and a gauging dock, to ascertain how much each boat would carry so that the correct toll could be charged, was built nearby.

Right: The last surviving building from the original canal basin. It was used as an office by Wigan Coal & Iron Company and was by Clarke's Basin. When the photo was taken in 2000, the coping stones from the edge of the basin were still visible under the cover on the left of the building. Today, the Marriott Hotel has been built on the basin site.

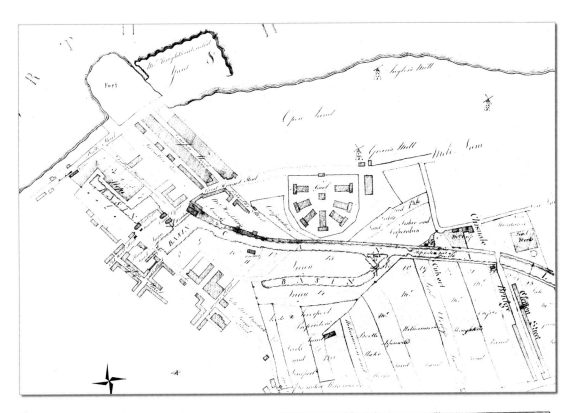

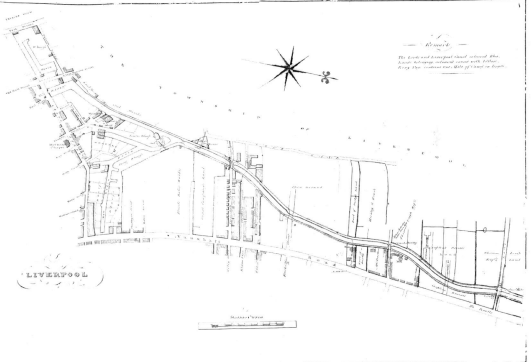

Two maps showing the terminal basin in 1802 and 1827. Note how new arms had been built to serve the coal and manure trades, and the warehouses for general cargoes.

By 1790 trade had increased to such an extent that an enlargement of the facilities at the basin was needed. A link to the river had always been part of the original plan but had not been carried out. The idea was raised again by the Dock Committee, while the canal company preferred a wagon way with shoots. Agreement could not be reached, and instead further coal wharfs were provided by extending the basin in 1792. Ladies Walk was purchased and the basin extended to Bath Street and the five new coal wharfs in Dutton Street. Old Hall Street crossed the entrance to this basin by a humpback bridge flanked by the new canal company offices. A further office was provided in Old Hall Street for the coal companies.

The area around the basin was becoming more and more built-up. Leeds Street, named after the canal, opened about 1790, shortly after Gibraltar and Dutton Streets were laid out. Great Howard Street, originally Mill Street as it led to Mr Green's and Mr Taylor's windmills, was extended, receiving its name from the philanthropist John Howard who was involved with the erection of the town gaol in 1786, near to the basin.

Merchandise traffic was increasing, though it never really flourished until the canal was opened throughout in 1816. The two earliest warehouses erected for its accommodation provided for the traffic to Wigan and that to Preston. The latter used the branch from the canal at Burscough down to the River Douglas at Sollom, reaching Preston by the Ribble estuary. It provided a safer and more regular route for goods than by trusting to the vagaries of the tidal passage round the coast. Warehousing was also provided by merchants in the surrounding streets where many also had their houses. The opening of the canal throughout brought major changes to canalside areas as industry and commerce thrived. Over time, merchants moved house to more refined districts in the east and south of the town, away from their warehouses, though the Blundell-Hollinsheads, a merchant family who had large interests in the canal, remained in the district until 1820.

Trade and Improvements

As traffic increased so did pressure on water space. Another arm off the canal was built on the east side of the existing basin in 1800 for the use of the timber trade and a second arm, built between 1808 and 1810, extended the basin system to Vauxhall Road. Clay underlies much of the land to the north of the town, and all that was excavated in building these arms was sold to local brickmakers. Their works were often adjacent to the canal where coal was easily available for firing the bricks.

The basin area was a hive of activity. Besides brickmaking and the timber yards, coal yards were operated by Mr Clarke, Mr Blundell, Peckover & Co., Hustler & Co., and several others, many of whom were both canal proprietors and owners of coal mines in the Douglas valley. A ropewalk was erected opposite the dry dock, convenient for supplying boatmen, and a white lead works had opened just beyond Chisenhale Street Bridge. The Bootle Waterworks, one of two private companies which provided the only supply of water to Liverpool until 1847, were located to the east of the basin in an area known as Pumpfields. Public services were also represented by manure wharfs, and for many years the town's refuse was removed by boat for use as fertiliser. Much was used to help reclaim and improve the wetlands of Martin Mere, in West Lancashire.

The canal was opened to Leeds in 1816 which led to an increase in traffic, the Union Company of carriers transferring its Yorkshire trade from the Rochdale Canal, opened from Manchester to the Calder & Hebble Navigation in 1804. Five years later the opening of the Leigh branch joined the Leeds & Liverpool to the rest of the canal system. Pickfords, after complaining successfully about the short locks on the Leigh Branch, were soon using the canal for a narrow boat service from the Midlands and occupied a warehouse at the basin for a short while. However, the long journey via Manchester and Leigh was inconvenient and they soon gave up, their cargoes being transshipped into flats at Runcorn for delivery via the tideway to Liverpool, a much shorter passage. Other large carriers, such as Kenworthy's, used the canal until 1842, when they gave up their warehouse following the introduction of railways. There were further extensions to the basin system in 1825, when a short arm was built towards Leeds Street, and in 1839 when an arm was built towards Vauxhall Road, parallel to Charters Street. This formed the maximum extent of the canal basin network, by which time over £60,000 had been spent on wharfs, warehouses and offices. The main offices for the canal were originally in Bradford where much of the original impetus for the canal came from. By 1850 trade in Lancashire was more important and, following the promotion of Mr Tatham from the Liverpool office to General Manager, the ca-

A typical example of courtyard to homes close to the canal terminal.

nal's head office was moved to Liverpool.

Social Conditions

By the middle of the nineteenth century the town's population was soaring. It had increased from under 50,000 in 1785 to 222,954 by 1841 and, with the growth of Irish immigration, sanitary conditions were becoming a problem. This was particularly so in the Vauxhall and Exchange Wards which encompassed the canal basin. Although few boatmen lived in Liverpool, being generally from the small towns and villages along the canal in West Lancashire, there were many relying on the canal for employment who lived near the basin. Among these were the coal heavers who unloaded the boats, working in gangs of four, each gang unloading eight boats per week, amounting to about 320 tons of coal. For this they received 3s. 8d. per boat each. In the 1860s they were described thus to a government committee by Mr Worsnop:

Coal-heavers are a very improvident class of men, and a very large majority of them seldom have a change of clothes for themselves or families. To give an instance of one who may be considered a decent fellow of the general run. He lives in a cellar at a rental of 2s. 3d. per week. He has a wife and four children. They are all clad in rags which are often filthy. The children are so small as to be unable to help themselves, and frequently are left for a day together without food or fire, and if it were not for the kindness of some of the neighbours who are far worse off in the matter of income, these poor children would be found almost starving, whilst both parents are off drinking.

Among the other canal-based trades were the night soil men. They collected the town's refuse and sewage which was then sent by canal to be used as agri-cultural fertiliser. Those loading these boats worked in gangs of three and were able to fill about six boats per week for which they received 24s. each (3s. per boat).

The consequences of living and working in such conditions were not widely realised until 1844, when Dr Duncan, who became Liverpool's, and the world's, first Medical Officer of Health, was examined by the Commissioners inquiring into the state of large towns. His figures showed that Liverpool had the highest death rate in the country. The average age at death was 17, with 1 in 28.75 of the population dying each year. The comparable figures for London were 26.5 and 1 in 37.38. The worst figures of all were for the district surrounding the canal basin. His investigations led to Liverpool's 1846 Public Health Act, another first for the city.

A year later the Council obtained an Act for improvements to the town's water supply. In the eighteenth century this had come from springs at Bootle to a waterworks near the canal basin, with other supplies being developed early in the nineteenth century. In 1847, two schemes were suggested. One used Lake Bala, the water being channelled partway towards Liverpool by the Llangollen Branch of the Shropshire Union Canal. This was the time when some canals were proposed for closure and conversion to railways, and this fate had been suggested for the Shropshire Union, though it was never carried out. Liverpool had to use their other scheme instead, the creation of a reservoir at Rivington. Much of the water came from the River Douglas, and consequently agreement had to be reached with the Leeds & Liverpool Canal who were responsible for navigation on the river. As compensation for their loss, sufficient water for ten locks per day had to be allowed down the river to feed the canal at Wigan, with further supplies to ensure that the tidal section of the river at Tarleton did not become silted.

Living conditions at this time were poor, with many houses used by the poorest sections of the community built in enclosed courts, and access was often through a covered passage under one of the houses. This meant that there was inadequate ventilation to the whole court. On top of this, many people lived in cellars, and as the underlying soil was clay and drainage was rarely provided, these often became flooded. There were few sewers and the middens provided instead often leaked so the conditions in such cellars must have been appalling. Besides the problems of

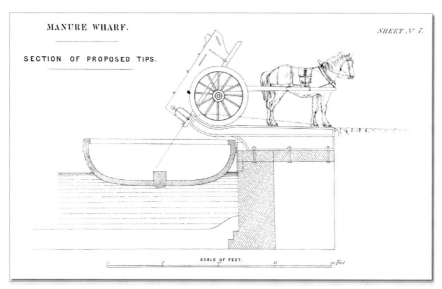

MANURE WHARF.

SECTION OF PROPOSED TIPS.

SHEET N.º 7.

SCALE OF FEET.

A tip for refuse designed in 1864 for the Charter Street manure and refuse wharf.

sewage, overcrowding was common, with seven or eight people often sharing a single room. Children were often sent to dame schools where little was taught and the overcrowding continued. Mr Wood described one in the 1830s as being

… in a garret up three pairs of dark, broken stairs, with forty children in the compass of ten feet by nine; and where, on a perch forming a triangle with the corner of the room sat a cock and two hens; under a stump-bed immediately beneath was a dog kennel, in the occupation of three black terriers, whose barking, added to the noise of the children and the cackling of the fowls on the approach of a stranger was almost deafening. There was only one small window, at which sat the master, obstructing three-forths of the light it was capable of admitting.

With such conditions fever broke out regularly and contagious diseases were endemic. Small wonder that the death rate was so high.

To combat the unhealthy conditions in the area the Northern Hospital had been set up in 1834. It originally occupied a house belonging to R.B. Blundell-Hollinshead at no.1 Leeds Street, where 20 beds were provided. Adjacent houses were taken over in 1836 and 1838, by which time 106 beds were available. These premises were soon insufficient, and in 1843 a purpose-built hospital was erected, backing onto the canal basin, next door to the gaol. The old site in Leeds Street became a weighing bridge office for coal brought by canal. However, provision of a hospital did not solve the problem of ill health, and

Dr Duncan, together with Mr Newlands the Borough Engineer, set about alleviating the cause by improving the disposal of refuse and night soil in a scheme which was to provide traffic for the canal for many years.

The Manure Traffic

There were three main types of refuse: street sweepings which included dirt and mud from the unmade roads, together with horse manure from the traffic using them; vegetable refuse, ashes and other household rubbish; and finally night soil. The first two were fairly innocuous, and could be collected at any time of day, though the ashes required picking over later to remove any clinker and coal which was then used in burning combustible rubbish. It was the night soil which was the problem. At this time, few sewers had been laid, and even the better class of house would have its own midden. These could leak, the liquor contaminating the immediate neighbourhood, especially any cellars. There was one bonus: the middens that leaked did not smell so offensively when they were cleaned out! This was only done on request, so many in the worst areas would not be emptied for months, with the inevitable consequences. When the scavenging department was asked to empty a midden this was done after twelve o'clock at night, hence the term night soil. However, many middens were situated in alleys which could only be reached with barrows. The night soil was then deposited on the pavement at the end of the alley for removal by horse-drawn cart, often late the morning. The refuse and night soil was then dumped on canalside wharfs to await sorting and loading before it could finally leave the town.

For many years the main wharf was at Phillips Street where there were three short arms, built in 1864, for loading boats. Other wharfs were at Burlington Street, Sandhills and at Harrington Dock, though Phillips Street was by far the most important. In the 1860s it was estimated that over 4,000 tons of refuse was removed weekly, while a further 3,000 tons of night soil was delivered to the canal wharfs. Here it was eventually loaded into boats and taken out to the farms of West Lancashire where it was used as fertiliser. It was certainly fortuitous that the soils there required this type of fertiliser and not the lime which the canal had originally been built to supply.

To cope with such an unpleasant cargo the boats were specially adapted; the planks lining the hold were caulked to make them watertight and an extra bulkhead was fitted at each end to give an air gap between the cargo and the boat's living accommoda-

Delivering manure in West Lancashire from the *Ben*. All such traffic had to be man-handled onto the canal bank.

tion. When the boats were being loaded it was not uncommon for manure to spill into the canal while the bilge water pumped out of the boats was described 'as of the foulest description'. Samples were analysed and found to be 68 times more noxious than normal sewage; small wonder that the canal company did not allow boats to be pumped out in the basin area where

The Charter Street destructor and its associated wharfs in 1906.

there was no flow to purify the water. Surprisingly Mr Tatham, the canal manager, stated that the 150 tons of mud dredged from the basin each week did not smell, attributing this to a reaction with the other refuse which fell into the water. Coal dust was also thought to purify the water, and considerable quantities must have fallen into the canal from Meyrick Bankes & Co.'s yard which was opposite the manure wharf. This suggested purification may well have occurred as later in the century charcoal was added to sewage in house middens and ashpits to reduce the smell. Tatham considered the neighbourhood of the manure wharf to be particularly healthy, though the Medical Officer of Health's mortality figures tell a very different tale. Earlier, in 1853, Tatham had moved from his house alongside the canal near the basin at which time he had complained that it was unhealthy. Perhaps he was not too worried so long as his own family was not at risk, though, to be charitable, his judgement may have been affected as he suffered a nervous breakdown in the late 1860s.

Railway Competition

The opening of the Bolton & Leigh Railway in 1828 and the Liverpool & Manchester in 1830 brought the first real opposition to the canal's trade, causing a reduction in tolls for goods to Wigan, Leigh and Manchester. However, it was not until the East Lancashire and Lancashire & Yorkshire Railways opened in 1848 to their station in Great Howard Street that the canal's income began to suffer from competition. Great Howard Street station was very inconvenient, as the canal basin effectively blocked access from the town. To overcome this the railways proposed to build a new terminus in Tithebarn Street, with their line into the station crossing the canal basin. Their plan entailed the demolition of the warehouses off Back Leeds Street, used by the Union Company for much of the canal's merchandise traffic, and there was considerable opposition. The basin was already overcrowded, and storage space for timber, stone and coal, all important traffics, would also disappear. There were further worries about fires caused by the locomotives. The canal company wrote complaining:

It may not be improper to observe that many of the goods which pass along the canal and which are necessarily exposed upon their wharfs continually are highly combustible, such as cotton, flax, oil, spirits, turpentine and even gunpowder, some of which articles railway companies refuse on account of the

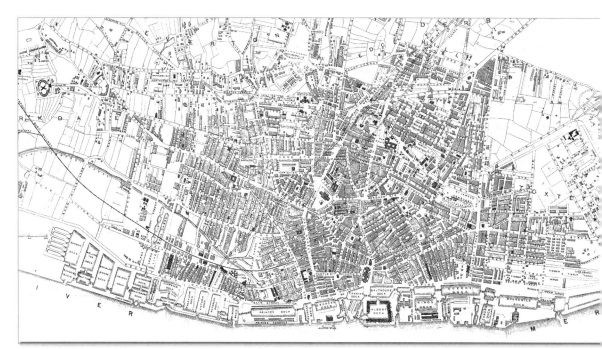

Liverpool in 1860, by which time the railway into Tithebarn Street Station had been built across the canal basin. Note that there had been little development along the canal to the north of the town. Such development awaited the opening of the northern docks.

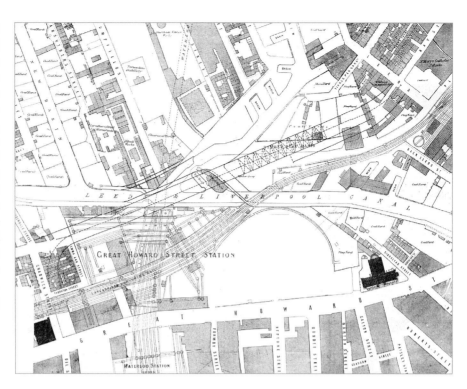

The 1878 plan for Pall Mall which required little alteration to the canal basin. By 1881, the scheme required much of the basin to be filled in, with Pall Mall providing a level route to the north of the town. (See p.34)

great danger there is from the sparks of fire which are emitted from their engines continually.

The business which was transmitted last year upon the wharfs proposed to be passed over by the railway was about 100,000 tons cotton, timber and general merchandise, 20,000 tons of flags, stone and bricks, and 8,000 tons of coal, all of which had to be carted either into or out of the town of Liverpool and for which these wharfs are conveniently situated.

The method of carting timber in Liverpool is by the means of wheels of great diameter to which the baulks, sometimes 60 feet long, are slung and dropped upon the timber wharf wherever the carter can find a vacant space and although the wharf is large it is frequently filled.

In spite of the opposition, the extension was approved but it had to pass over the basin on a viaduct, missing the warehouses and thus reducing any interference to the canal's trade.

One result of competition for trade between the railways and the canal was that merchandise-carrying on the canal was leased to the railway companies for 23 years from 1851. This caused a reduction in the tonnage carried on the canal, though it brought in a guaranteed income. Following representations from many East Lancashire merchants in the early 1870s,

unhappy about the service given by the Lancashire & Yorkshire Railway, the company decided to revive merchandise-carrying.

As a result considerable improvements were carried out all along the canal to facilitate cargo handling. At the basin new offices and a warehouse were built on Old Hall Street in 1873. The following year a steam crane was installed on the timber quay. This must have been successful as steam engines, each powering several cranes, were soon fitted in the main warehouses. Merchandise traffic increased rapidly, from 285,261 tons carried 11.61 miles on average in 1873, to 499,545 tons carried 29.74 miles in 1880. In 1877 a large investment, over £3000, was made in providing a provender store, veterinary services and stabling for the company's horses. It was located at 35 Leeds Street, at the corner with Tinklepeg Lane, and was leased by Joseph Leather and Sons, veterinary surgeons, in 1879. It was soon to be demolished in radical changes to the area.

Pall Mall

For many years the Town Council had been concerned about the poor road system to the north of the town. The canal basin effectively blocked the way, and though it was possible to use Old Hall Street,

Boats and boatmen await cargoes alongside the warehouses on Pall Mall. Note that the boat on the left has entered an arm off the basin. There were several arms into the warehouse, each one designated for a different destination – Blackburn, Bradford, Leeds, etc. – with flyboats departing daily at 6.00pm.

The entrance to the offices in the 1950s after they had been destroyed by an incendiary bomb during the Second World War.

the humpbacked bridge over the arm to Clarke's basin made it difficult for heavily loaded horse-drawn vehicles travelling to and from the northern docks and the new industries which had developed on the canal banks. To solve the problem they proposed to build a new road through to Love Lane. At the same time the Lancashire & Yorkshire Railway wanted to enlarge their station in Tithebarn Street. Because the canal had to be crossed, this had been built at a high level so the public had to ascend stairs to the trains.

The L&YR goods yard in Great Howard Street in 1913. It was built on the site of the old canal basin, the girder bridge on the left originally carrying the railway over the canal. In the background are the canal warehouses on Pall Mall, with the canal's offices on the right.

They wanted to build a new entrance which would improve access.

Initially these two schemes were separate, the railway's being proposed in 1876, while the Corporation obtained its Improvement Act in 1878. This allowed the extension of Ray Street by a new street, Pall Mall, on which the basin was crossed by a bridge. Some demolition of canal property would have been necessary, and the dry dock filled in, though a new dry dock and boat yard had been built in Wigan for the maintenance of the company's growing fleet of boats, which numbered about 100 in 1880. In 1881 all three parties got together and agreement was reached for a slightly different scheme. The canal basin was to be filled in to the west of the extended Pall Mall and sufficient land sold to the railway for their development.

There were several good reasons for the canal company's agreement: despite modernisation, many of their facilities were old-fashioned; their finances were always tight; and their household coal trade, much of which used the western side of the basin, was declining as railways opened small coalyards in the suburbs. At the time the basin handled annually around 60,000 tons of manure, 60,000 tons of stone and building materials, 87,000 tons of coal and 104,000 tons of merchandise. The scheme would provide them with modern warehouses, equal to any the railways owned, while the land released would give them a regular source of income from rents or sales. Work was soon in hand and the old terminus closed in August 1886. The tenants of the old basin were compensated for the inconvenience and arrangements made for new premises. Wigan Coal & Iron Company, perhaps the largest coal supplier on the canal, moved from their yards in Back Leeds Street and Carruthers Street to a new site on Commercial Road. This was certainly smaller than before and, as they required no compensation for the loss of a 24-stall stable, suggests that their household coal trade supplied via the canal was declining.

New warehousing was built along Pall Mall and can still be seen, though that erected in Leeds Street was pulled down recently when the road was widened. The alterations and new warehouses cost some £50,000, though the company received over £100,000 as compensation, thus making a considerable profit. At the same time a three-storey office was built in Pall Mall by Roberts & Robinson at a cost of £7,908. Besides the usual boardrooms and toll office

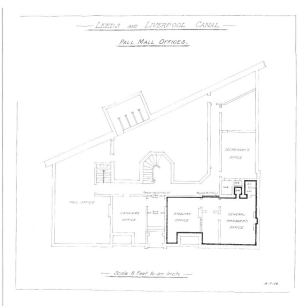

The ground floor of the offices. Upstairs were the engineering department and the boardrooms.

needed by a canal, there was an engineering drawing office and a freight office for the company's fleet of boats. These offices were destroyed by bombing during the Second World War, though fortunately many of the company's legal records had been moved to a strongroom built at Bank Newton maintenance yard, near Gargrave, while the traffic office had been re-established at Blackburn.

The moral welfare of canal workers in Liverpool was not neglected when the Liverpool & Wigan Canal Mission was established by Mr & Mrs Wood in 1864. Financial support was received from the canal company, who also provided premises at the basin. There certainly seems to have been an improvement in conditions, Moses Jackson of the Mission complaining in 1876 to the Secretary of State about George Smith's tirade on the poor conditions endured by boatmen:

This I am bound to deny and am assured by all the residents near the canal between Liverpool and Wigan that within the last twelve years the transformation which has taken place in the boat people is really wonderful – in cleanliness, language and general conduct.

He went on to say that 50% could read, only 20% could be classed as drunkards, and not more than 1% were living as man and wife unmarried. Most had homes on the bank and at least 50% of the children

Above: The warehouses on Leeds Street, seen here in 1979, were demolished when the street was widened in the 1980s.

Left: Boatmen pictured outside the Boatmen's Mission on Pall Mall.

went to school. Much of the change in attitudes had resulted from the influence of the Mission. From 1878 the Mission moved to the old canal offices and, in 1891, they amalgamated with the Mersey Mission to Seamen. New premises on Pall Mall were built in 1908 and were extended the following year, at the boatmen's suggestion, by the provision of a small shooting gallery. Obviously many boatmen wanted to keep their poaching skills sharp whilst in town! The Mission closed in the mid-thirties. It has since been demolished but part of the frontage on Pall Mall remains. In 1905 the Mersey Mission to Seamen had taken over the old Liverpool & Wigan Canal Mission in New Lane, Burscough. As St Andrew's Mission, it remains in use today, the last Canal Boatmen's Mission in Britain still in use as a place of worship.

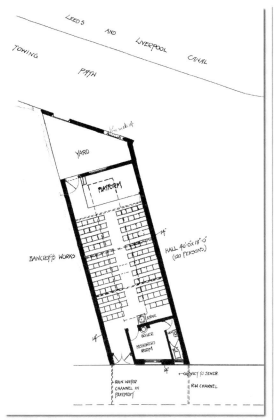

The floor plan of the Mission. There was no doorway onto the towpath to prevent unauthorised access to the canal.

More Manure

The manure and refuse traffic continued to thrive as the population grew. The construction of sewers was progressing and consequently sewage was becoming less important as a cargo. However, this was more than offset by the increase in household refuse. Carr Hall Farm, near Burscough, had been purchased by the Corporation in 1871, and 90,000 tons of refuse was dumped there over the following three years. Local farmers complained and the dumping ceased, the Corporation instead paying canalside farmers about 9d. per ton for permission to discharge refuse unsuitable for manure on their lands. This class of refuse was the most difficult to dispose of, so in the early 1880s two steam hopper barges, *Alpha* and *Beta*, were purchased to take the refuse out into Liverpool Bay, where it was dumped beyond the bar. *Alpha* worked from the South Docks while *Beta*, which could carry 400 tons, was loaded in Collingwood Dock by hand from canal barges. This was found to be very slow, so to improve matters new iron canal barges were built to carry 24 steel-framed wooden boxes, each box taking about 2 tons of refuse. These were loaded at the canalside refuse depots and then delivered to the docks where they were emptied into the hopper barge. It took twenty minutes to unload each canal barge using this system, which employed just four men instead of the thirty-odd needed previously.

Refuse containers being loaded at Sandhills wharf before being taken down to Collingwood Dock for transshipping to one of the hopper barges.

Beta **whilst loading in Collingwood Dock.**

Better ways of disposing of rubbish were continually being sought, and in 1891 a 12-cell destructor was installed at the Charters Street wharf. Two years later it was enlarged by a further 12 cells. In these cells the refuse was burnt, its weight being reduced by two-thirds, and the resulting ash and clinker used to make paving slabs and mortar. Electricity was also generated and used to light the surrounding area, whilst the waste steam was used to disinfect contaminated clothing.

The manure traffic to canalside farms was to continue well into the 1940s, only declining as more and more houses were connected to the sewerage system. In the 1860s there were complaints about manure remaining on the wharf in Liverpool and creating a health hazard. To overcome this the Corporation purchased manure wharfs in West Lancashire, subsequently insisting manure should be loaded directly into boats in Liverpool and only stored on those wharfs outside the town. In theory the manure was only allowed to remain for seven days maximum at these country wharfs but this was often disregarded. The tonnages carried were immense with over 7,000 tons being delivered to one wharf in Lydiate in six months. Well over 100,000 tons was removed from Liverpool annually. The boatmen were paid on the tonnage carried and in 1904 the Lancashire Farmers Union at Ormskirk complained that dry manure was dampened with canal water by the boatmen to increase the weight, sometimes by 10 or 15 tons. The added water could have made the manure considerably more offensive and Mr Tomlinson, a Burscough JP, complained in 1884 about the state of the local manure wharfs:

It is monstrous that such accumulations should be tolerated in the midst of such a populous village. Honest horse and cow manure deserves respect, but the villainous compounds that are positively ennobled by being styled 'manure' reek with noxious odours that send one home to Sunday dinner many a time with a sickened appetite.

The manure certainly had a bad reputation, though this was well deserved by all accounts. The boatmen involved in its carriage did not usually complain of the smell, but those on other boats always tried to keep out of their way and loathed having to follow one of the manure boats.

Many of the manure wharfs can still be found in West Lancashire, often located near bridges. This is the one at Halsall, as with several others now converted into a car park.

Electric Power and the Twentieth Century

The year 1897 saw the purchase, by the Corporation, of the Liverpool Tramway Company. It was decided to electrify the system and one of the two power stations built for the system was at Pumpfields, adjacent to the canal. Twelve Willans vertical type compound triple expansion engines were installed producing 15,000hp, generating electricity at 460–500 volts DC. This was used for street lighting as well as for the trams. Coal, brought by boat, was unloaded onto a conveyor belt running parallel to the canal and feeding a hopper. A second conveyor then led to the boiler house. The canalside site had the added advantage that the canal could be used for cooling the condensing water, though this was to have an adverse effect later.

In 1912, St Paul's Eye Hospital moved to Old Hall Street, and it eventually occupied the former offices of the Wigan Coal & Iron Company. Even after the hospital had closed in 1992, it was still possible to see the coping which formed the edge of Clarke's Basin at the back of the building. Amongst other companies to lease buildings on the old basin site was Guinness, who occupied former canal warehousing on Old Hall Street for many years in the twentieth century.

Following the First World War, during which government policy had seriously damaged the profitability of canals, the Leeds & Liverpool decided to give up its carrying fleet. From 1921 this was sold piecemeal to various byetraders. They also gave up their warehouses, those in Liverpool eventually being sold

The electric power station in 1990, shortly before it was demolished.

Chisenhale Street Bridge in 1935, showing the effect of cooling water from Tate & Lyle's on the canal.

to the Mersey Wharfage Company in 1927, though preferential treatment there was ensured for canal carriers. In 1936, by which time they had become the Liverpool Warehousing Company Ltd, they were complaining about the condition of the canal water. Tate & Lyle had installed new plant which relied upon the canal for condensing water, and this together with the Corporation electricity works was raising the temperature of the water excessively. In November they wrote:

During the last couple of days visibility in the yards has been nil, causing loading operations by crane and warehouse hoist to be dangerous.

Men certainly cannot work under prevailing conditions without serious risk to their health, one man is, in fact, absent from duty with chest trouble, certainly aggravated by the continuous damp conditions ...

Goods in store are of course badly affected, and

although we have succeeded in disposing of parcels of cattle cake damaged by surface mould, I am nervous that a time will come when this contamination will be noticed.

The canal company complained to Tate & Lyle's who subsequently erected cooling towers to remove most of the heat before water was let back into the canal.

The Second World War caused considerable interference to the canal. The Liverpool section was closed for six months following major bomb damage at Sandhills. The Head Office was also destroyed by bombing, though the warehouses survived. As in the first war government was loath to provide canals with the financial help received by railways, and this, combined with the demise of traditional canalside industry, brought about the final decline of canal carrying. Boats had ceased to use the basin for several years when, in 1960, it was filled in as part of the redevelopment of Tate & Lyle, bringing to an end almost two hundred years of canal transport in central Liverpool.

The Basin Area Today

Today there is a surprising amount left, considering the recent wholesale changes to the city centre. Perhaps the most important is the name Leeds Street, and the layout of the small streets here can also be related to the old canal basin. Apart from that, remains of the terminal basin before the 1880s reorganisation are few. Only the former coal office used by Wigan Coal & Iron Company survives in Old Hall Street, though it is now overshadowed by the Marriott Hotel. A listed building, it became incorporated in the Eye Hospital, which closed in 1992. It is the only building remaining from this period of the canal's history. The bridge over the canal was not removed until twenty years after the basin was closed, being used as a cellar for the adjacent buildings. Clarke's basin and coal wharfs disappeared when King Edward Street was built across the site in 1904. Thomas Bennett & Co.'s cooperage expanded into the area from their original premises in Brook Street, but these too have now disappeared together with the warehouses in Bath Street which were pulled down about forty years ago.

Warehousing in Leeds Street was demolished around 1990 when the road was widened, with the warehouses on the corner of Pall Mall being demolished in 2004 for the construction of a car showroom. In Pall Mall itself much of the warehousing remains, together with the warehouse foreman's house. A 1960s office occupies the space left after the canal's head offices were destroyed during the war. The canal company name can still just be seen painted on the old gable end of the surviving warehouses here. On the other side of Pall Mall, one abutment of the railway bridge which once crossed the old canal basin can still be seen, a reminder of the days when Scottish expresses steamed out of Exchange Station.

The water space behind the warehousing is now used as a car park, with copings and mooring rings

Bomb damage to the canal opposite the Bank Hall coal tip, with several badly-damaged coal boats. *Guido*, on the left, was owned by John Parkes and was rebuilt, continuing to be used into the 1950s. The canal was reopened within three weeks.

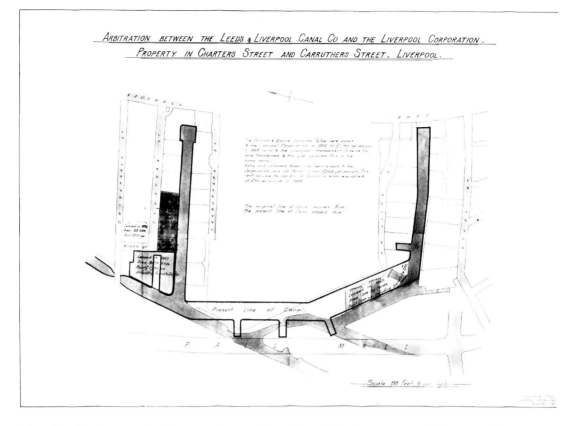

The plan for the new basin, superimposed on the old basin, as agreed during arbitration between the canal, railway and council in 1881.

still visible. On Pall Mall, towards Chisenhale Street, can be seen the frontage of the Boatmen's Mission, built on the site of the old toll office. In Chisenhale Street itself the canal bridge remains alongside the former Bridge pub. In the streets surrounding the arms off the main basin a few old buildings survive, though most were directly connected with the canal. The largest building here was the old Pumpfields Electricity Station, but this was demolished in the 1990s.

Pall Mall in 2007, with the site of the Boatmen's Mission in the foreground, and the surviving canal warehouses beyond.

A view of the basin from Leeds Street in 1984 after the warehousing had been demolished for road widening.

3. DOWN TO THE MERSEY

Liverpool in the mid-eighteenth century was fast developing into the main English port for trade with the American colonies. The woollen merchants of Bradford saw great opportunities in these markets and the Leeds & Liverpool, it was hoped, would improve access to raw materials and for shipping their goods to the colonies. One advantage of canal traffic is that canal boats can transfer cargoes to and from seagoing vessels directly, without using wharfs or quays. To capitalise on this a clause was inserted in the canal's first Act authorising a branch linking the canal to the river, thus enabling such transshipment to take place. Unfortunately Liverpool's Town Council, through their lease and subsequent purchase of the township lands from Lord Molyneux in 1671, controlled the foreshore. They also owned the dock system and so could restrict the opportunities open to the canal for a branch to the river or for a connection to the docks. Such a link was often suggested in the years following the passing of the canal's first Act in 1770, but it was not until 1846 that one was finally constructed.

In earlier times, local government and industry had been dominated by the interests of titled landowners, but both Liverpool and the Leeds & Liverpool Canal were precursors of a new age where decisions would be made by merchants rather than landed gentry. Until the mid-nineteenth century, when Parliament began to take more interest in local government and the co-ordination of industry and transport, this resulted in 'small-town politics'. These were much in evidence in the dealings between the fiercely independent merchants of Lancashire and Yorkshire, and were to delay the construction of a link between the canal and the docks.

A Link with the River

The Town Council had supported the initial promotion and surveys for the canal, but when the canal's Act was passing through Parliament they ensured that a clause asserted that only they could construct a branch into the dock system and that

a link to the river, separate from the docks, was all that could be built by the canal. This attitude of the Council was to prevail for the next seventy years, despite the problems it would cause, and as a result the canal had to change the site of its scheme for a branch to the river repeatedly to avoid new docks as they extended northwards.

After the 1770 Act had been obtained, work in Lancashire was concentrated on constructing the canal from Liverpool to the Douglas Navigation so that coal could be supplied to the town from Wigan. The committee decided to hold the river link in abeyance until after the opening of that section of canal. By mid-1774 this was open, but as it had cost far more than expected, a wagonway, cheaper to construct, was suggested as a link between the docks and the canal basin. There was still the possibility of a branch, but the Town Council warned that the 1770 Act did not allow this to join their new dock, and that the line should be moved further north so as not to interfere with dock extensions.

A year passed with no solution to the problem, though Mr Eagle, the canal's solicitor, was asked by the committee if their Act gave authority for the construction of the wagonway. The company's problems were increased when the War Office decided at the end of 1775 to build their new barracks and fort for the protection of the port on the very piece of land earmarked for the branch. Despite these setbacks arrangements went ahead for the branch, coal yards being located on the eastern side of the canal basin so as not to interfere with construction. A committee was appointed to confer with the Town Council in the hope of financial assistance for the scheme, but there may have been local ill-feeling against those controlling the canal in Yorkshire. The Liverpool men may have decided to get their own back for the Yorkshire proprietors' intransigence over the canal route through Lancashire, and insisted on the letter of the Act which required the company to pay for the construction of the branch.

At the beginning of 1776 they then complained

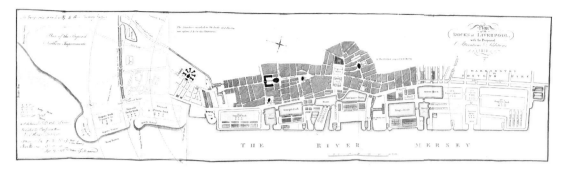

The 1810 plan for a link between the canal and the proposed Princes and Regent's Docks. The plan was not carried through, construction work concentrating on the southern docks which were not as easily accessible for canal traffic.

that the line proposed interfered with their new dock works and asked for it to be moved 100 yards to the north. Henry Berry, the Dock Engineer, would then check this line and produce a plan agreeable to the Council. They also insisted that a bridge be built on the road along the shore where it would be crossed by the canal. By April the canal company, whose finances were virtually exhausted, again asked for financial assistance in building the branch. This the Council refused, reminding the canal that they must make all the works at their own expense. They also disagreed with the new scheme, though they seemed averse to explaining why. The canal company then replied demanding recompense for having to alter their Parliamentary line. The two sides must have agreed to postpone building the branch, but we shall never know definitely as the canal company minutes are missing for the following month, as are those of the Town Council. Relations improved as eighteen months later Henry Berry was allowed to use the clay originally purchased by the canal for the branch for a road to the new fort. It was considered superfluous as the existing links to the docks, by horse-drawn wagon, were to be continued.

Coal Port

Merchandise had been the main reason behind the initial proposal for a dock branch, but when three plans were presented to the committee, in 1787, for a canal into the Mersey, it was the export of coal which was foremost in the promoters' minds. The idea of making Liverpool into a major coal exporter was resurrected several times in the following sixty years. On this occasion it was probably brought about by the decision of Lord Balcarres, the main Wigan coalown-

er, to develop the export of his coal and cannel to Paris. He had some success, but not enough to warrant a new dock and branch.

The Act for Princes Dock was passed in 1799, and a branch from the canal basin was proposed to the new dock. In 1802, Fletcher, the canal's engineer, set out a line for the branch, and the Council were approached as their consent was needed. No further action was taken, and construction of the dock was postponed, the southern docks being developed instead. It was not until 1821 that Princes Dock was opened, the suspension of work on the northern docks adversely affecting the canal. When a Bill for the improvement of the southern docks was presented in 1811, the canal company petitioned against it, stating that Princes Dock should be built first. They were concerned that goods interchanged between the canal and the docks, which were transported by horse-drawn wagons, had to cross the town to reach the southern docks, a much longer and more expensive journey than to the northern docks. Mr Hustler, one of the Wigan colliery owners, wrote to the company complaining:

The principal part of our sale is with Ireland – considerable to America, and the coasting vessels to Wales etc, at present vessels so employed find births in the three west docks, viz. Georges Dock, the Old Dock, and Salthouse Dock, and for coasters, the bason near the fort; and the cartage to those places is very reasonable say from 1/- to 1/6 per ton.

He went on to say that any increase in transport costs would make coal from Prescot and the Sankey more attractive to purchasers to the detriment of the canal's trade. With Princes Dock so close to the canal basin, it would materially reduce the congestion and expense caused by such traffic. A compromise was

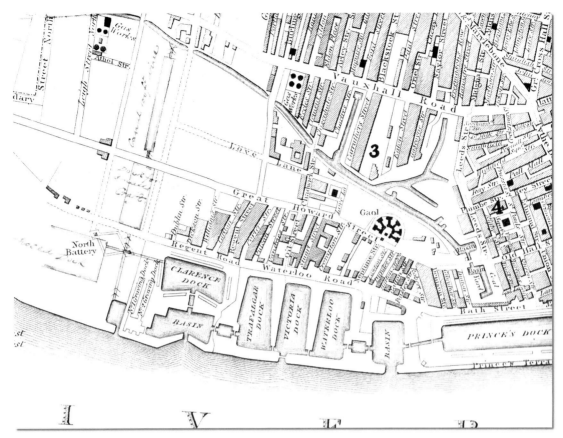

An outline plan for an 1844 scheme to link the canal to the proposed new northern docks. This became the Stanley Dock scheme, the line of the canal as built being moved slightly to the north.

eventually reached in which the time for completion of the dock works, both north and south, was extended, though there were still doubts as to the availability of berths in the south docks for small coasting vessels in the coal trade.

Two years later the canal company proposed to build a dock and basin, to be called Regent's and Derby Docks respectively, for these vessels, on land to the north of the unfinished Princes Dock. The scheme was drawn up by William Chapman, a London engineer, who surveyed four lines between the canal and the river, two from the basin and two from the canal. He preferred one from near the basin which would descend four locks into a dock 270 feet by 110 feet which could accommodate six of the vessels then used in the coastal coal trade. Coal yards would line one side of the basin, which it was hoped would handle 120,000 tons annually. However, the Dock Committee asked too high a price for the land required and the plan was shelved. The scheme for a branch to

the river was not abandoned, and in 1825 the company had a clause inserted in a new dock Bill which allowed them to move its position to the north, thus avoiding the northward extension of the docks.

The Stanley Dock Branch

In 1834 there was an abortive proposal for a branch into the recently opened Clarence Dock, then in 1843 the Dock Committee contacted the canal company suggesting that a link could be built to their proposed new works. The scheme was included in their 1844 Act for the extension of the northern docks. Several schemes for the canal link were drawn up by Jesse Hartley, the Dock Engineer. In one Stanley Dock was omitted, the canal emerging directly into Collingwood Dock, whilst another had a dock running inland from the eastern end of Stanley Dock parallel to and to the south of the branch. This was resurrected in 1857 and again in 1872, though nothing came of it and a large wool warehouse was eventually built

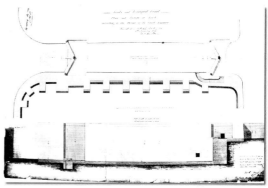

The lock house at the top of the locks, now demolished, was where traffic through the locks was controlled from.

Jesse Hartley's design for the canal locks. The masonry on the locks is typical of his work, and is of high quality. Built by the Dock Board, the branch was immediately sold to the canal company.

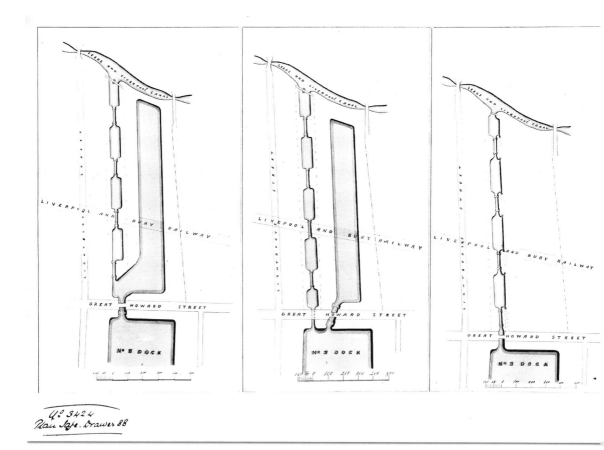

Three designs for the branch between Stanley Dock and the canal. The inland dock was for coastal craft, and though the idea was raised subsequently, it was never built.

From Canal into River.] 165 11.34

MERSEY DOCKS AND HARBOUR BOARD.

CERTIFICATE as to destination of Cargo of Coals, or other Goods or Commodities, now on Board the Flat or Vessel called the
of which   is Master, about to pass from the
Cut communicating with the LEEDS AND LIVERPOOL CANAL, through or into the Stanley Dock, required to be made in order to obtain the Exemption of such Cargo from the duty of Three-halfpence per Ton, under the Mersey Dock Acts Consolidation Act, 1858, Sec. 236.

We, the undersigned, being the Owners of the said Cargo, do hereby certify and declare that it consists of   tons of

and is actually intended to be Shipped *on board the*   being a
sea-going Vessel, now lying in   *Dock, and about to sail on a*
Voyage to   ON BOARD OR FOR THE SOLE USE OF THE STEAM-BOATS
CALLED
BEING STEAM-BOATS PLYING ONLY WITHIN THE RIVER MERSEY, OR PORT OF LIVERPOOL.; and we declare that this Certificate is issued *bona fide*, and with our full knowledge of the facts herein stated, and that any untrue statement contained herein, will subject us to the penalties imposed by the Dock Acts on the Evasion of Dock Rates.

Dated this   day of   19

NOTE. *In the cases to which the words in italics apply, those in small capitals must be struck out, and vice versa.*

Left: A permit to use the locks and thus gain access to the docks. Some canal traffic was exempt from charges by the Dock Board (MDHB), but some had to pay for the use of the dock wharfs.

with the Dock Board. At first coal was the main traffic and in 1851, three years after the branch had opened, 303 boats delivered coal from Wigan to the docks, 134 to Cheshire, 7 with wheat from George's Dock to Blackburn, 6 with timber from Toxteth Dock to Accrington and 4 with flags from Burnley to Birkenhead. There were many more small cargoes besides. The collection of tolls ceased from 2nd December 1960 as by then there was insufficient traffic to make it worth while.

Traffic to and from the docks developed rapidly, and more branches were suggested, although none were ever completed. In 1850 the old plan to link the basin with Princes Dock re-emerged. The canal company were not very keen on the idea, which was designed in particular for coal traffic. It was to run from the end of the basin in Batho Street. Four years later the Dock Board proposed a branch canal into a new dock they were planning. This was one of the early schemes for Canada Dock in which six small docks and two large timber docks were to be built, the latter on reclaimed land. There were also to be five graving docks. It was suggested that this dock system could be connected to the main canal by four locks, possibly built as a single four-rise lock, on a branch parallel to Castle Street in Bootle. Again, the canal company were not enthusiastic, and insisted on a six-mile minimum toll. They were also concerned to limit the depth of the locks to eleven feet to reduce

on the site. The canal was to be built by the Dock Board who would then sell it to the canal company for £50,000. The scheme was costed on a canal line slightly to the south of that actually constructed, on the line of the inland dock proposals noted above. The canal as built required slightly more land as the canal gently turns away from the docks at this point. In the event, some of the land between Great Howard Street and Regent Road was retained by the Dock Board, reducing the price to £42,622. The exact charge for the land created problems in accounting, and put back the final payment for the work by the canal company until 1851. The canal company provided outline plans for the locks but they were built to the design of Jesse Hartley, and show masonry typical of his work on the rest of the dock estate. He was ill at the time of construction, and his son, John, was responsible for the actual building work.

A lock house was built by the canal company at the top of the locks, and men were employed round the clock, Monday to Saturday, by the Dock Board to control the movement of boats to and from the docks. There was a toll on goods which had not paid dock dues and certificates giving the load carried by each barge from which this was calculated were collected by these men. In 1855, the main canal was widened around Leigh's bridge because of the number of boats waiting for locks. The locks could be used on Sundays, though prior arrangements had to be made

The *A40*, a motor canal boat built in the 1930s for carrying grain, is seen here crossing the Mersey.

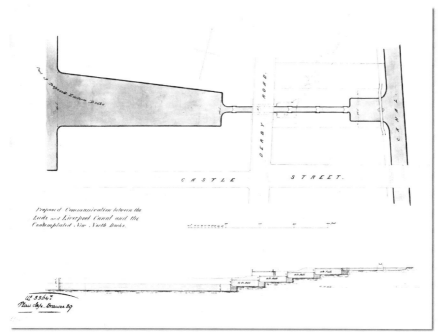

Proposed Communication between the
Leeds and Liverpool Canal and the
Contemplated New North Docks.

One of the 1884 schemes for connecting the canal to the new northern docks. Instead new warehouses were built at Bankhall and Bootle, with goods being carried to and from the docks by horse-drawn lorry.

the water usage. The scheme was linked to the creation of a coal port and the High Level Railway into Bramley-Moore Dock. Wooden coal hoppers carried on railway wagons were part of the scheme, and it was suggested that these could be transshipped onto floats in the canal at Liverpool and carried down the locks and into the docks. Blundell's and MacKay's collieries in Wigan were already using hoppers, and

the scheme would have further reduced the volume of coal carried from Wigan, and cut the canal's income.

Improved connections with the docks were suggested on two further occasions, in 1864 and in 1884. On the former occasion it was thought that a new wharf and warehouse at Sandhills would serve just as well. Warde-Aldam, one of the directors, wrote of

Grain was carried by canal boats from the silos in Birkenhead Docks across the Mersey and on to flour mills along the canal.

the wharf:

It is very favourably situated for cartage traffic to the docks. The vessels going down the locks only communicate with 2 or 3 docks, but this wharf communicates, within a very short distance, by Sandhills Lane into the Regent Road, which runs along the line of docks. Whether for coal, timber or stone it is very convenient for traffic with the docks.

One of the problems with canal access was that the docks did not all interconnect at that time. For boats to pass along the line several tidal basins had to be crossed which made the trip time-consuming. This was why wharfs on the canal were considered a better means of communication, as the increased costs of transshipment were offset by speed of delivery. Tidal basins made access to the docks easier for large sailing craft. As steamships became the norm, the tidal basins were removed, improving access for canal boats and to some extent removing the need for new branches. However, after George's Dock was filled in at the start of the twentieth century for the redevelopment of Pier Head, canal boats had to be towed in the river between the north and south docks. For moving boats in the river, particularly to Birkenhead, the canal company had its own steam tug, *Warrior*, built in 1885 by Messrs W. Allsupp of Preston for £2,500. It was sold to W. Bate & Co. in 1921 after the canal company gave up carrying.

There was one more attempt to build a second link to the docks. In the 1890s plans were drawn up for a branch running parallel to Balliol Road down to Brocklebank Dock. There were to be two sets of two-rise locks, with space for boats to pass between. It was hoped that the scheme would reduce the time taken for canal boats to reach the most northerly docks, but there was probably insufficient traffic to make the expense worthwhile.

Around the Branch

A short arm was built for the Bridgewater Canal below the first lock in 1856. The Bridgewater's depots were all in the south docks and this basin and warehouse were to serve vessels in the more recent northern docks. Canal companies usually had problems co-operating especially, as here, where they were in competition. There were arguments about the tolls

Liverpool Locks in the 1950s, with a dredger on the left and maintenance boat on the right. Note the industrial nature of the branch, with the oil tanks on the far side of the canal's main line at the top of the locks.

The wool warehouse, by this time with access to the canal bricked up. Wool was an important canal cargo, with extensive canalside warehouses being built for the trade in Shipley and Keighley in the 1930s.

charged for the use of the few metres of canal necessary to reach the Bridgewater's warehouse, the two companies ending up in court before a compromise was reached. The depot proved expensive for the Bridgewater and they had vacated the premises by 1910.

There had been little development of the Lightbody Street area prior to the construction of the branch. The land to the south was owned by the Dock Board, and workshops for the maintenance and construction of docks were built here shortly after the branch opened. These became less important as the docks progressed northward and in 1895 they were replaced by a large wool warehouse. Wool for delivery to Yorkshire was a major traffic on the canal, and the company suggested that an arm should be built from the branch into the new warehouse. The Dock Board would not entertain this and instead raised gangways were suggested to enable bales to be carried over the towpath and then lowered into boats underneath.

Between the canal and Lightbody Street were several small yards. During the nineteenth century most were occupied by slate merchants, many Lancashire

roofs being covered with Welsh slate carried by canal from Liverpool. By the end of the century this traffic had been taken by the railways who could deliver without the need to transship, thus reducing breakage. In their place were coal yards, the chemical works of G. Hadfield & Co., and the Anglo American Oil Co.'s stores. Hadfield's remained there for many years producing artificial fertiliser. The oil stores were expanded during the twentieth century and Shell Mex and BP also had premises here by the 1930s. The Dock Board built a canalside refuse destructor at 38 Lightbody Street where rubbish from the docks was burnt which for many years was operated by the Bootle Barge Company, owned by the Caddick family who were canal boatmen for several generations.

Today the arm has changed completely. Over the last ten years or so, housing has been built on both sides of the canal, and access has been radically improved. The locks remain, and after the canal link across Pier Head opens, they will be used more often. Until recently, several retained the older type of paddle gear which has disappeared from locks on the main canal. The canal into Liverpool is a 'remainder

Above: Bootle Barge Company's yard at Lightbody Street, with some of the assortment of barges and boats they owned in the 1970s. Their destructor for burning refuse and paper is in the background.

Right: The canal today offers a very different sight to the time when it was a hive of industry.

Below Right: The pump house at the bottom of the locks. It was unused for many years, but new pumps have now been installed to compensate for the water used by boats passing through the locks to the new canal link across Pier Head.

waterway' so for many years it was difficult to find money for adequate maintenance. Also to be seen at the bottom of the locks is the brick shed housing the pumps formerly used to back-pump water from Stanley Dock into the main canal. These were installed in 1934 when there was concern over the supply of water to the Liverpool Pool in summer, the River Douglas, the main supply, being heavily polluted. The construction of the Hoscar water treatment works in the 1980s has resulted in much cleaner water from the Douglas supplying the canal today.

4. INDUSTRIAL DEVELOPMENT AND THE CANAL

Tate & Lyle's sugar refinery, seen here in the early 1960s after their extension had been built over the entrance to the canal's terminal basin, is typical of the industries which flourished on the canal's banks. Not only did the canal provide transport, but also cooling water, though here cooling towers had to be built because the temperature of the canal became too high.

Liverpool in the second half of the eighteenth century was one of the major manufacturing centres of Lancashire, and it was the need for a supply of coal to industry that was the main reason behind the promotion of the canal in the town. Compared to the rest of Lancashire the local merchants were well established and considered themselves more refined, the phrase 'Manchester men, Liverpool gentlemen' reflecting this view. They were less inclined to have their environment polluted by industry and, for this reason, a copper refinery had been forced to leave the town. This attitude, together with the rise in land values and increase in wages brought about

by the success of the port, resulted in a decline in the importance of manufacturing industry in the town and the rise of service industries such as food processing and packaging.

In the early nineteenth century, industry tended to be located near to the docks, though there were a few canalside factories built in the years after the canal opened. It was not until the rapid growth of the northern dock system in the mid-nineteenth century that there was significant canalside development as dock extensions opened up the north of the town. It is possible the the canal and its terminal basin may well have had some bearing on the slow extension of industry northward as they

Old Hall Street looking towards the town centre when the canal bridge was being removed in 1902. Arthur Guinness & Son were then occupying warehouses built on the old canal terminus, and the canal office which still survives today was just off the photo on the right.

created a barrier to the easy movement of road traffic between the town centre and the north. Certainly the humpback bridge over the canal in Old Hall Street was a continual source of traffic congestion until it was removed early in the twentieth century. The construction of Pall Mall in the 1880s was also designed to improve road communications to the north of the town, partly by removing the old terminal basin.

A further bar to Liverpool's development northward was the independence of the township of Bootle. It was not until late in the nineteenth century that Liverpool finally realised that it was unlikely to incorporate Bootle in its boundaries. Until then, there was an area with little housing or industry between them.

The nineteenth century saw great changes on the canal banks. Farming was important when the canal was built, and the local hunt kennels were also close to the canal. Agriculture declined steadily, being replaced by housing and industry. Even the location of these altered over the years. Because of the complex-

Boundary Street Bridge marked the division between Liverpool and Kirkdale. Rebuilt in 1861, the bridge still bears the marks of bombing during the Second World War.

ity of the development along the canal corridor we will look at which industries were in operation there at the beginning, in the middle, and at the end of the nineteenth century. The rise and fall of the Liverpool chemical industry took place during this period, and there were many canalside sites.

The primary role of the canal during its first fifty years of operation in Lancashire was to supply Liverpool with coal. This was delivered to an ever-increasing number of coal wharfs around the basin from where it was transported by road to factories and docks. Several industries soon transferred to sites alongside the canal where coal could be supplied directly. Soap, glass and chemical factories were especially keen to move to such sites in the undeveloped northern part of the town where their pollution would be less problematical.

All three industries were based on alkali. This was imported in its naturally occurring forms of barilla, kelp or potash, from which it was then extracted. Soap making was, perhaps, the most important of the three industries, Liverpool rivalling the traditional production centre of London by the start of the nineteenth century. The town's soft soap industry, which used vegetable oils imported from the colonies, soon came to dominate the market. The process created much waste soda which was then used in glass bottle making. Besides soap and glass manufacture, alkali was increasingly used during the processing of textiles, with vitriol (sulphuric acid) and bleaching powder (from chlorine) being produced at canalside factories. Pollution from reactions using these chemicals, as we shall see later, became a major disincentive to the development of the industry in a heavily populated town. The chemical industry developed because the rapid increase in the demand for alkali by the soap, glass and textile industries required a synthetic product, that available naturally proving inadequate. Besides coal delivered by the canal, the ease of supply of salt from Cheshire was an important factor in the decision to locate the industry in Liverpool, salt being one of the basic raw materials for the production of synthetic alkali.

The Canal in 1800

In 1800 the canal approached Liverpool through agricultural lands, with only the occasional factory. The first to be noticed was just before the bridge at Litherland Road in Bootle, then known as Stamp House Swing Bridge, where the Bootle Glass House could

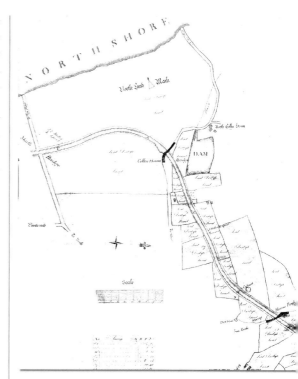

Bootle in 1802, with the Glass House almost off the map bottom right, close to Stamp House Bridge. The Coffee House and mill dam are top right, close to Bootle Land Mark, one of the guides for shipping in the river.

be seen across a field to the south. Bootle springs, from where water had been piped to supply Liverpool from 1799, could also be seen across the fields. After passing through Stamp House Bridge there was a tan house for curing leather to the west, but the surroundings were still predominantly agricultural. Before the next bridge the Bootle Coffee House could be seen to the north beyond the dam and lodge which supplied water to the waterwheel at Bootle Mills where there was also a windmill. Just before leaving Bootle there was a potash house between the canal and the foreshore, used to the supply the soap industry which was developing around Liverpool.

The canal continued through farming land, past Bank Hall and Vaux Hall, the next industrial site being Messrs Moore and Gouthwaite's glass bottle works. This was located at Gerard Bridge, almost opposite where the dock branch was built forty-six years later. Next to the works was a windmill for grinding corn, operated by the Halewood family. There were many windmills in Liverpool at this time, and the milling industry was a major user of the canal throughout its working life.

The canal now passed through open land until Chisenhale Street Bridge where Mr Porter had recently opened his lead works. After the bridge the terminal basin was reached. The Bootle Waterworks Company's yard and reservoir between the canal and Vauxhall Road was fed by a pipeline from Bootle springs. A steam pumping engine was used to supply the town, the area becoming known as Pumpfields. Other steam engines were already established in the area, Bateman, Greaves & Co. having been allowed to use the canal water for their engine from 1791. There were other industries, such as soap and chemical works, round the basin, while a cotton mill, known as Union Mill, was being operated by Messrs Kirkman & Co. on the east side of Vauxhall Road. This was unsuccessful and was later taken over by Messrs G. Forrester & Co. for use as a foundry.

Developments by 1850

In 1800 George's Dock was the furthest north the dock system reached. By 1850 eleven more docks had been built and work was progressing northwards on Sandon and Huskisson Docks. The Lancashire & Yorkshire and East Lancashire Railways had also entered the town by a route almost parallel to the canal. Much of this development had occurred over the preceding ten years and was to radically change the canal corridor as industry and housing followed. Gas lighting, introduced to Liverpool in 1815, was also to provide further traffic to the canal as works were erected alongside.

Industry now reached as far out as Litherland where a tannery had been built five and a half miles from the basin. A second tannery in Litherland, known as Ashburners, reflects the importance of the dairy industry in the locality. In the days before refrigeration milk had to be delivered quickly and most towns had a thriving dairying community on its outskirts. As early as 1775 the canal company had complained about cattle grazing on the towpath, such trespassers being impounded in West Derby pinfold. Litherland also boasted an asphalt manufacturer and two sandstone quarries, all of which used the canal.

Bootle Glass Works had now been converted to chemical manufacture and had moved alongside the canal at Bootle Bridge. The waterworks was still operating, but seems to have been the only other industry in the area, though much residential development had taken place between Coffee House Bridge and Bank Hall. The northward progress of the docks had

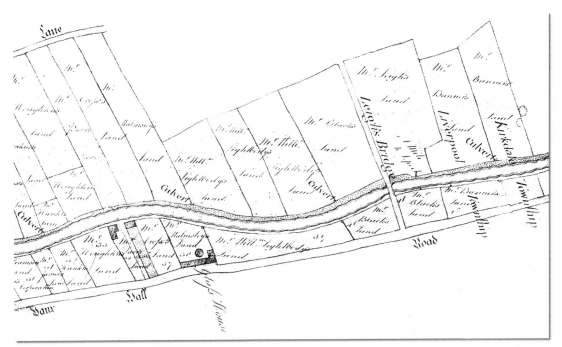

The glassworks site, on Vauxhall Road close to Leigh's Bridge in 1802. This was one of the first industrial sites to develop alongside the canal in Liverpool.

North Shore Mills around 1900. Most of the boats here are the deeper dumb barges, unsuitable for the canal beyond Bootle, which brought grain from storage silos in the docks. In the background is a canal boat which has brought coal for the mill's boilers.

not yet reached Bootle, where many Liverpool merchants lived in houses overlooking the estuary. The prevailing westerly winds made this a much pleasanter place than Everton to the east, which suffered from windblown industrial pollution from the canalside chemical works.

At Bank Hall were the Lancashire & Yorkshire Railway locomotive sheds, water for the engines being taken, by agreement, from the canal. A siding alongside also allowed goods to be transshipped, though it is uncertain how often this was used. After passing under the railway there was a tile works, the underlying clay to the north of the town being ideal for brick and tile manufacture. The kilns were fired with coal brought by boat from Wigan.

No more development had occurred until Bounda-

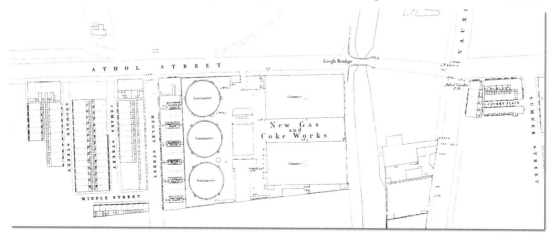

Athol Street Gasworks in 1848.

ry Street, marking the division between Liverpool and Kirkdale, was reached. Here the North Shore Cotton Mills had been erected around 1840. As with other Liverpool textile factories, it only survived for a few years. After standing empty for a short while it was converted into the North Shore Flour & Rice Mills and was the first of several large modern steam-powered flour mills to be built alongside the canal.

At the next bridge, Athol Street, was the Liverpool New Gas and Coke Company's works, opened in 1834. This company had originally been set up as the Oil Gas Company in 1823, producing gas from whale oil. Later other oils, such as palm, linseed and herring, were tried in an attempt to reduce costs, though gas produced from oil was more expensive than that from coal. Costs had to be reduced as they were in competition with the Liverpool Gas Light Company, set up in 1815 to supply gas from coal and who had been operating from canalside works at Eccles Street, near Burlington Street, since 1829. The Athol Street works allowed the New Company to compete with the Old until 1848 when the two merged to form the Liverpool United Gas Company. The Eccles Street works closed in 1934 while production at Athol Street continued until conversion to natural gas around 1970.

Although their product was called coal gas, it was generally produced from cannel. Much of this came from the Wigan Coal & Iron Company's pits at Haigh, though later their pits at Crooke and Maypole were the main suppliers. In 1849 approximately 30,000 tons were delivered to Athol Street. Four years later a severe winter caused problems in delivery when the canal froze. Instead the cannel was sent to Sandhills by rail where it was transshipped into barges for final delivery. Although the coal company did not have a legal claim for the recovery of their losses, the gas company paid the following bill for their additional expenses.

Additional cost of conveying 1945 tons of Cannel from Haigh to Sandhills Bridge per Railway: 97– 5– 0

Additional cost of Hauling of Boats of Cannel from Haigh to Melling with extra horses and men: 47–17– 3

Hauling the said boats thence to Gas Works and boating 1945 tons from Sandhills: 111– 9–10

Estimated damage done to boats: 180– 0– 0

Loss of horse drowned: 50– 0– 0

479 tons of large cannel sent in lieu of small to gain time @ 2/- 47–18– 0

£534–10– 1

The gasworks wall in 1990, showing the many gates which once provided access to the works. Today, housing has been built on the site.

The Athol Vaults is the oldest surviving building in the area.

The demand for gas, mainly used for lighting at this time, was at its highest during the cold, short days of winter, and large quantities of cannel were needed. It was vital to keep the canal open if at all possible, though disruption of traffic because of frost was to remain a serious problem for the canal company. In Liverpool this was alleviated because the canal was used as a source of cooling water by canalside industries, resulting in this section rarely being troubled by ice in the late nineteenth and early twentieth centuries. However, by the 1960s the decline of canalside industry had reduced the need for cooling water and during the hard winter of 1963/4 the canal froze for many weeks. Because of this canal traffic ceased and the carriage of coal to the gasworks was transferred to the railways. It did not last long, as the introduction of natural gas resulted in the closure of the gasworks.

The land between the canal and Vauxhall Road was slowly being taken over by a variety of industries. Opposite the gasworks were four that were typical. R. P. Gardner & Co. operated a seed-crushing plant probably supplying the growing demand for animal feedstuff. Nearby was Kerr & Mather's steam sawmill, timber being a major Liverpool import with considerable quantities passing along the canal. The sugar industry, long established in Liverpool, was represented by Crosfield, Barrow & Co.'s refinery, while both Fredrick Wedekind and J. T. & A. Fairrie had refineries further along Vauxhall Road. In 1850 Henry Tate was still a retail grocer with five shops, one of which, in Old Hall Street, was near to the canal basin. In 1859 he became a partner in the firm of John Wright and Co., sugar refiners, in Manesty Lane, and it was not until 1870 that he built his innovative refinery in Love Lane, near to the canal. The last of the four representative industries was John Blanchard's flour mill, the grain and flour trade beside the canal being long established.

Muspratt's Chemical Works

Along Vauxhall Road, opposite the flight of locks down to the docks, were several coal wharfs, mainly supplying the domestic market. Beyond these was the extensive chemical works of James Muspratt & Son. This site had originally been occupied by the glassworks of Gouthwaite and Moore. James Muspratt, a chemist from Dublin, arrived in Liverpool in 1822, setting up as a potash and vitriol producer on this site the following year. He was soon making soda ash by the Leblanc method in which salt is reacted with vitriol to produce alkali (sodium carbonate). Although he was not the first to utilise this process, the lead-lined tanks he constructed to hold the acid were, at 112 feet long by 24 feet wide, many times larger than any in use at that time.

Initially the manufacture of synthetic alkali was little understood, which resulted in considerable pollution. The sulphate waste produced was originally dumped near the works, but later was taken away by boat. Methods were eventually discovered for re-

Coal being delivered to the gasworks in the 1950s. Note how industrialised the banks of the canal had become. Today grass and modern housing has replaced the industry.

The notorious chimney of Muspratt's chemical works.

claiming much of this sulphur. More of a problem was the muriatic (or hydrochloric) acid gas produced by the reaction of salt with vitriol. The initial solution was to build high towers to allow the gas to be carried away on the wind. There were two at Muspratt's works, one of them 250 feet high and built in 1835. Unfortunately these just seemed to spread the pollution further, Muspratt being prosecuted more than once for creating a public nuisance.

One case came to court in 1838 in which it was claimed that the gas killed plants and trees, tarnished brass and changed the colour of dyed cloth. The health of those living locally, particularly in Scotland Road and Everton, was also adversely affected. There was a suggestion by some friends of Muspratt that the gas improved health, the prosecution replying facetiously:

But it will be said … that this is a most kindly gas, this muriatic acid gas, that it is exceedingly beneficial, and that, were it not for Mr. Muspratt and his fellow alkali manufacturers, the town of Liverpool would be poisoned.

The prosecution then called 49 witnesses to testify to the damage brought about by the gas. Despite a spirited defence, Muspratt was found guilty and fined, though the works continued in production. It would have been virtually useless to close just one factory in the hope of improvement as at that time there were 12 chemical works, 23 distilleries, 17 soap works, 16 breweries, 7 lime works, 17 foundries, 2 gasworks, tan yards, 3 sugar houses, 3 colour factories, 5 waterworks and 13 steam mills and mortar mills in the area surrounding Muspratt's. The abatement of one source of pollution, even though it was a serious one, would have had little beneficial effect on the immediate environment.

James Muspratt originally found it difficult to sell the 'black ash' produced by the Leblanc process as the local soap manufacturers seem to have been reluctant to replace natural potash with his synthetic article. It has been suggested that he had not only to give it away but also to supervise its use in soap-making. However this reluctance was soon overcome and the works continued in production until his death in 1886. By this time he also had factories in Widnes and Flint, his son Edmund becoming the president of the United Alkali Company on its formation in 1890. The site, which included eighteen cottages and a shop, was sold to the canal company in 1887.

There were three more factories between Muspratt's and Burlington Street Bridge: the distillery of Archibald Walker and two sugar refineries, first Wedekind's then Fairrie's. Through the bridge was Vauxhall Gasworks, while on the other bank was the rice mill of Carstairs & Co. with the Clarence foundry behind. Tenements begin to make their appearance,

Poor-quality housing was found throughout the Vauxhall area.

51

Burlington Street Bridge during reconstruction in 1904. Liverpool Oil Mills are on the left, with Atlas Warehouses in the distance. The arm to the right served one of the many corporation manure and refuse wharfs.

a large block having been erected by the Council between Chisenhale and Charters Streets. These were an improvement on the poor quality housing to be found elsewhere in the Vauxhall Ward.

At the basin, besides the coal and manure wharfs, were several more chemical and soap works. Of particular note were William Hill on Vauxhall Road and Thomas Lutwyche on Pumpfields, both of whom had been producing synthetic alkali before James Muspratt though on a small scale. Another well-known chemical manufacturer, Charles Kurtz & Son, had premises on Carruthers Street, while Thomas Hadfield's chemical works were on Pumpfields. Besides these chemists there were soap manufacturers, oil merchants, boiler makers, flour millers and a host of smaller businesses clustered round the canal basin. Many operated day and night, and with the continual passage of coal wagons and manure carts the area must have been a hive of activity.

The Twentieth Century

By the turn of the century the dock system was virtually complete. Only two more docks were to be opened, Gladstone in 1927 and Royal Seaforth in 1972. Urbanisation had continued apace, and there was now no interruption to the houses and factories lining the canal between Liverpool and Bootle, while the nearest green fields were as far out as Linacre. This development, together with an acceleration in the pace of life, had led to considerable increases in road traffic. There were many complaints about the humpback bridges over the canal which were causing problems for the heavily laden horse-drawn wagons passing to and from the docks. These bridges were the property of the canal company who were not interested in their improvement. It would be costly, and money needed to be spent helping traffic on the canal rather than the road. Instead the local authorities in Liverpool and Bootle agreed to finance bridge reconstruction, taking over the expense of maintenance. Consequently most of the bridges in the area were enlarged, their approaches improved and their carrying capacity increased in the years around 1900.

Where the canal company did invest was in the provision of improved warehousing. As has been mentioned before, the basin area was totally rebuilt in the 1880s when Pall Mall was lengthened, new offices and warehousing being provided at the same time. Previously a new warehouse had been erected in 1874 at Bank Hall, boats entering this via a short arm so that they could be loaded under cover. The cranes used for lifting goods here were operated by a small steam engine located next door. It was built by R. & J. Rankin & Co. with a 9in diameter piston and 16in stroke operating at 60lbs/sq in with steam from a Lancashire boiler 14ft long by 4ft 6 in diameter. By 1891 this had been replaced by hydraulic power. Further warehousing, costing over £18,000 and opened in 1885, was provided at Carolina Street in Bootle. This became the centre of a small canal community, several boatmen living in the streets nearby. Extensions to the warehouses continued into the twentieth century.

Because of the congestion in town centres, industry was beginning to think about moving to more rural sites. In 1920 it was proposed to build a National Aircraft Factory between the Old Roan and the racecourse but the decline in post-war armament produc-

Bank Hall Bridge was rebuilt by Robert Dagleish of St Helens. It is seen here around 1902 with the canal warehouse of 1874 in the background, where a steam boat and an unpowered dumb boat have just been loaded.

tion removed the need. Not long afterwards Liverpool Corporation Electricity Department suggested that they would build a power station at Aintree, but

Bootle warehouse in 1986. Two arms off the canal entered the warehouse so boats could be loaded under cover. The terraced housing of the Carolina Street area has been replaced by new houses behind the warehouse, which was itself demolished around 2002 for new housing.

Melling Pottery was one of the few canalside factories in the Aintree area.

again this came to nothing.

Twenty years earlier industrial development still only reached as far out as the canalside tannery at Litherland. The asphalt factory had closed and, possibly as a result, there had been an increase in housing. This caused growth in road traffic, creating problems for the swing bridge keeper at Litherland. In July 1894 the Clerk to the Local Board wrote complaining:

The writer had occasion to call the attention of the person in charge of the bridge for detaining the traffic for a considerable period until there was an absolute block about a week ago, and we understand that on Saturday last the bridge was drawn for about twenty minutes, and a considerable number of vehicles of all description were congregated on both sides of the canal, but in justice to the man on the bridge he did his best to close the same, but the people in charge of the boats would not stop to allow him to do so.

He certainly seems to have been in a better mood than a month later when the Clerk again complained:

On the writer coming to town on Saturday morning he observed this bridge drawn to permit of a canal boat passing through which was some distance away, and on the slope of the hill a heavily laden waggon was standing about six yards from the bridge, and it was with difficulty the horse could keep the waggon in position. The writer pointed out the absurdity of drawing the bridge and keeping a laden waggon standing within a few yards of the bridge and the only satisfaction he got from the canal company's caretaker was the abrupt reply 'You just mind your own business'.

Crossing the canal here was to remain a problem, though the wooden bridge was replaced by an iron one in 1908, built in Garston by Francis Morton & Co. and carried by canal boat from Garston Docks to Litherland. The barge was ballasted, the bridge perching precariously on top of the gunnels, the overall clearance only just allowing passage through the bridge under Great Howard Street near Stanley Dock. A lifting bridge replaced the swing bridge in 1934, in its turn being demolished in the mid-seventies when a new overbridge was constructed to improve road access to the Royal Seaforth Dock.

In 1900 there were still a few open fields near Linacre Gas Works. This had been opened in 1867 and was to become one of the largest in the area. Its reliance on the canal for supplies was reduced during the First World War when two carburetted water gas plants were opened which used imported oil as their raw material. However, gas continued to be produced

The replacement swing bridge at Litherland with the original bridge-keeper's cottage behind.

Calder **passing under the 1934 lift bridge c.1960.**

Left: Linacre gasworks in 1947. The Pine Grove destructor can be seen bottom right, with the chimney of Williams' toffee works bottom centre.

great demand in Liverpool. Most canal boats used in Liverpool were built or repaired in West Lancashire where wages were lower and jobs scarcer. There was, however, a boatyard in Canal Street, near Coffee House Bridge, operated for many years by the Skinners. Another, at the terminal basin, disappeared when Pall Mall was built. In the 1930s a new one opened when Parkes converted an arm at Bank Hall into a dry dock for the use of their coal boats, and this continued in use until coal traffic ceased in 1964.

Around the boundary between Bootle and Liverpool numerous terraced houses had been built by 1900, many on roads leading up to the canal, and footbridges crossed the canal to provide easy access to them. There were an abundance of small works as well. Amongst these were several timber yards including a clog sole and wood fibre factory in Ensor Street and a match factory on the opposite canal bank. Both needed regular supplies of timber. Numerous warehouses had been built alongside the canal as well, but it is uncertain if their trade relied on boats. There was another chemical works at Bank Hall with R. S. Hudson's dry soap works opposite the canal warehouse, while on the other side of the bridge was Bank Hall Oil & Chemical Works, with the coal tip for coal brought by rail just beyond.

Through the railway bridge the North Corporation Yard had been built, where rubbish and manure were loaded into boats and railway wagons for delivery to

from coal in part of the plant into the 1960s.

The chemical industry still survived. There was an alkali factory next to the gasworks and a soap works almost opposite. Adjoining this was a sack and bag works, the first of several near the canal. There was also Bootle's manure wharf and Pine Grove refuse destructor, manure and night soil being dispatched to West Lancashire by Corporation owned canal boats even after the Second World War. Just after Stanley Road bridge there were Appleby's corn mills. The firm, based at Enfield, near Accrington, had several other mills in East Lancashire and owned a large fleet of boats for carrying grain to them from the docks.

There were few boatyards on this section of the canal, probably because shipwrights were always in

Right: Parkes' *Bembo* passing under the new Coffee House Bridge in the 1930s. A coal-loaded boat heading out of Liverpool was unusual, so *Bembo* has probably been loaded with coal at Bank Hall tip for delivery to Linacre gasworks, and has just passed Skinner's boatyard.

Murillo at Parkes' boatyard, Bank Hall. After floating over the slipway, Murillo has been lifted out of the water by winches which raised the ends of the slips. She will then be pulled along the slipways onto hard ground on the right for repair.

West Lancashire farms. On the site next door, originally the Derby Coalyard, a printing and carton-making factory was opened in 1904 for the long-established Bolton printing firm of John Tillotson. Cartons were printed, cut and folded, particularly for the tobacco industry. Their main customer was the British & American Tobacco Company, whose large factory was to be found alongside the canal between Sandhills Lane and Boundary Street. This site had been the Vauxhall Gardens before a variety of foundries and corn mills took over. All, with the exception of Bee Mills on Boundary Lane, were demolished for the new factory. Tillotsons was extended in 1934, at which time two-thirds of its production was for the cigarette trade, though soap and food packaging

The Bank Hall area in 1986, with the canal warehouse and Parke's yard centre. The open space is Canada Dock Goods Yard after all railway track had been removed. This was the site of the wartime breach caused by bomb damage.

Coal being tipped from a railway wagon at Bank Hall.

By the time this photo of *Kennet* was taken in the 1950s, the oil and chemical works at Bank Hall had been replaced by railway sidings. *Kennet* is loaded with coal for either the gasworks or Tate & Lyle.

North Corporation Yard around 1900, with horse-drawn wagons tipping refuse into container boats. The containers were unloaded into steam hopper barges in Collingwood Dock and the refuse dumped in Liverpool Bay.

BAT and Tillotsons factories in 1986, with Bank Hall warehouse just visible in the distance. By this time most of the railways serving the docks had been closed.

demands were increasing. The factory is one of the many to have been demolished around 1990 following closure.

At Boundary Street the Liverpool North Shore Rice & Flour Mills were still in production, while at Athol Street there was a new development, the works of the Liverpool Hydraulic Power Company, erected about 1885. Steam-driven pumps pressurised water, which was circulated through the centre of the city

Comet loading sugar at Tate & Lyle's Love Lane refinery in the 1950s.

by underground mains. Four pence per 1,000 gallons was paid for canal water to fill the hydraulic mains as well as the canal company's annual standard charge of 10s. per engine horsepower for condensing water, used to increase engine efficiency by condensing exhaust steam. The company provided hydraulic power for lifts, presses and a variety of other uses for many years, closing down in the 1960s.

Nearer the town centre there were more changes, with warehousing, bottling stores, flour and oil mills having been established. At Burlington Street we come to Tate's sugar refinery. Henry Tate, son of a Chorley Unitarian minister, had come to Liverpool in 1832 to learn the grocery trade. By 1859 he had six shops. To expand his interests he became a partner in John Wright's sugar refinery, selling his shops two years later. In 1869 the partnership was dissolved, Tate continuing alone and building a modern new refinery in Love Lane, backing onto the canal. It opened in 1872 to become one of the country's most successful refineries, being continually expanded as land and opportunity allowed. In 1921 the firm amalgamated with Abram Lyle & Sons of Greenock to become Tate & Lyle, subsequently taking over the Liverpool firms of Fairrie & Co. in 1929, and Macfie & Co. in 1938. The acquisition of other industrial sites in the area enable the company to develop their works until it occupied both banks of the canal. One of those, leased in 1950, was that of the Corporation's Burlington Street open-air baths. Perhaps these did not pay as many lads preferred to go 'skinny-dipping' in the canal.

When the terminal basin was abandoned in 1960, this too was partly taken over and developed, a new warehouse being built on the filled-in bed of the canal. However, following the decline in the use of sugar cane as a raw material the works have closed and been demolished, the Eldon Street housing development now occupying much of the site.

By 1900 most of the industry near the basin had declined. The Corporation destructor and its chimney, demolished in 1952, dominated the surroundings. The Corporation were also responsible for the electricity station built on Pumpfields to supply the new electric trams. The moral welfare of the neighbourhood was catered for by All Souls Church, opened in 1856. A school was built alongside later. Today most of the old buildings have disappeared. There are, however, a few old workshops still to be found.

Skinny-dipping at Burlington Street Bridge in the mid-1890s, with Vauxhall gasworks in the background.

Demolition of the Charter St. destructor chimney in 1952. In the background can be seen the canal basin warehouses with their overhanging canopies and a train entering Exchange Station.

5. PEOPLE, PACKETS AND PLEASURE

The building of the canal was financed privately and it remained private property until nationalisation in 1948. Even then the towpath did not become a public right of way, and it was not until recently that it has become legal to use it as a footpath. From the earliest days there were problems with people trespassing. In 1777 the company minutes noted:

Whereas several complaints have been lately made by the owners of land contiguous to the said canal navigation, of great damages being committed by disorderly, idle people breaking down the fences, destroying the herbage of the land, and fishing in the canal. Also by persons riding upon the towing path and turning cattle loose upon the banks contrary to the Act ...

Notices were printed to confirm that the canal was private property, but the public continued to ignore them. There were even occasions when horse-drawn carriages were found using the towpath in order to evade turnpike dues. The canal also continued to attract those bent on leisure and in 1790 there were further complaints:

... of unqualified persons drawing nets in the canal and of disorderly idle persons breaking down the banks and fences and drawing the clows under pretence of fishing ...

The canal company was concerned about interference with the water supply, but it was the landowners who complained about fishing as in the Canal's Act they were entitled to any fish caught.

The problem resulted from the ease of access to the towpath, every bridge providing an unobstructed way of entry. Swing bridges were built originally, but over the years these were replaced by stone arches. When the canal was first built there were only seven bridges between the basin and Litherland, more being installed as the area developed. Between Litherland and the Old Roan, where the swing bridge was replaced in 1787, the opposite has happened. Originally several occupation bridges were provided to link farm property divided by the construction of the canal. Most

have now disappeared, the sale of fields isolated by the canal making them unnecessary. On these occupation bridges gates were sometimes provided to stop cattle wandering onto the towpath.

The bridges could also be a problem if boatmen failed to close them. The Earl of Sefton complained to the canal company in 1803 that the bridge at Aintree which he used to reach home was often left open, causing him great inconvenience. Ever anxious to appease the local aristocracy, a cottage was built by the company at a cost of £53 and Handcock, a canal employee, installed to look after the bridge, which is now known as Handcock's Bridge.

Access to the towpath at the terminal basin was unrestricted, and particularly easy from Old Hall Street. Following the building of Clarke's Basin there were several drownings late at night. To overcome the problem the company fixed a chain around the water's edge which was removed during the day when boats were loading and unloading, and replaced at night to prevent accidents. The company also provided lamp brackets, though they asked the local Commissioners of Watch, Scavenging & Lights to provide the lamps.

Trespass on the towpath in Liverpool was to remain a problem. In 1916 the company replied to a request by the Corporation for gates controlling access to the canal at Chisenhale, Burlington, Lightbody, Athol, Boundary and Bankhall Streets and at Sandhills Lane, enquiring whether the gates should be solid or of open construction so that the police could see onto the towpath. They noted that:

The bridges which are the property of the Corporation with in some cases open and comparatively low parapets are a source of trouble to those using the canal and for the protection of boatmen and others the Company ask that the Corporation should erect closed parapets not less than five feet high, in order to prevent mischievous children from throwing missiles at passing horses and boatmen as is now the case. The gravel boxes especially that

Lightbody Street bridge in 1956 when this small motor tractor was being tested for towing boats on the canal. Access to the towpath from Lightbody Street was through a locked steel door. J. Walker is driving, watched by C.S.R. Hall, Traffic Manager North West and Mr Pugh of J.G.Pugh Ltd, owners of the tractor.

at Bankhall Bridge should also be removed further away from the canal as they supply ammunition for boys and others to throw at passing boats and much gravel is thus deposited in the canal.

The gravel would have been used to help horse-drawn traffic pass over the canal bridge in icy weather.

Gates seem to have been fitted about 1930, presumably fastened with the canal company's hand-cuff lock which would allow any company employee or boatman to open them. Someone must have left Lightbody Street gate unlocked in 1933 when a teacher from St Sylvester's School took a party of children along the towpath to reach the lock fields which they used for games. This had been forbidden as it encouraged children to use the towpath. The school later apologised to the company, explaining that the teacher was new and was unaware that he was trespassing.

To prevent the towpath becoming a right of way the company observed a 'halfpenny day' each year when everyone using the towpath was charged that

Bid to cut city canal toll of life

THE Leeds and Liverpool Canal banks at Bootle and Litherland are to be surveyed by experts with a view to carrying out proposals designed to reduce child deaths through drowning.

The experts will report to a joint conference of interested authorities next month. This was decided at a meeting in Bootle yesterday called jointly by the corporation and Litherland Urban Council.

Five children have been drowned this year, and in the Netherton area alone twenty lives have been lost in the last nine years.

Representatives of the Ministry of Transport, the British Transport Commission, who own the canal, and Lancashire County Police attended the Bootle meeting.

Bootle has spent £12,500 on a six feet high iron fence one and a half miles long, but children slip through the gaps at the swing bridges.

A cutting from the *Daily Post* in September 1959.

amount for the privilege. The money was collected by the maintenance men, receipts being given after 1903 to avoid trouble, as on one occasion previously two women had started to beat one of the men with their umbrellas as they thought he was begging. The custom died out about 1920 when cast-iron notices were fixed forbidding cycling and trespassing. These slowly disappeared, legal requirements being served by printed notices pasted up once a year.

Although the canal had always been both an attraction and a danger spot for children, public concern about safety increased in the late 1950s as traffic declined. Bootle Corporation installed lifesaving equipment in 1958 though it was continually vandalised. The end of coal deliveries to the gasworks came in 1964 and three years later the section from Old Roan to Liverpool was closed to commercial traffic. Twenty-six children had been drowned there over the previous twelve years and there was a strong campaign by local MPs to have the canal filled in and converted into a road to the docks. It would have been too expensive and nothing was done, though there were several reports produced on access and safety. As slum clearance took effect the problem moved further out to the new housing estates at Ford and Netherton. They were erected with little thought to the canal running through their centre which was isolated by high fences. Today there is a more enlightened attitude which encourages the use of the towpath by adults whose presence can restrain children. Pleasure boats are again beginning to use the canal into Liverpool, but years of problems with vandalism have given this section a bad name amongst today's boaters. Things were different when the canal first opened.

Packet Boats

Packet boats, for the carriage of passengers and small items of goods, seem to have commenced between Liverpool and Wigan almost as soon as the canal opened. The company charged one halfpenny for every two miles travelled by each passenger, who was allowed fourteen pounds weight of luggage free. The bookkeeping associated with the packets may have proved difficult as the following year they were charged a single fee of £90 per annum per boat. There were two operators: Longbotham & Co. and the Union Company, whose boat was owned by Messrs Chadwick & Co. In 1776 another operator, Mr Ellison, commenced operations, his tolls being at the old rate of a farthing per person per mile. A cheap

rate of a halfpenny per return trip was introduced the same year for passengers travelling from Liverpool to Crosby Races.

Trips to the races, which became a regular feature of packet boat operation, reflect the intense local interest in sport. In the eighteenth century the Corporation maintained its own kennel of hounds for hunting, for many years housed between the canal and the foreshore near Bank Hall. Ormskirk Races were also served, return tickets in 1808 costing 1/6 in the fore cabin and 1s. in the back. Aintree Racecourse developed right alongside the canal. Originally there was no fence on the canal bank so many people used to watch the racing from boats or the towpath. In 1924 the King watched the race from there with Lord Derby, who later thanked the canal company for organising this. It must have alerted the Tophams, the course owners, to a source of lost revenue as the following year they leased the canal bank, though it was not until the 1950s that they erected a fence. Although this stopped the view from the towpath, people still came by boat for the Grand National, and several of the local carrying firms fitted grandstands to their boats for the occasion. Today the tradition continues and there are often a few pleasure boats in attendance on race day.

The company took over the operation of the packets in 1782 after the Union Co. had found it difficult to make them pay in winter. They seem to have been built with two cabins divided by a kitchen in the centre, which served food to the first-class passengers in the fore cabin. There was accommodation on the roof, used in fine weather or when the cabins were full. The boats were usually well over sixty feet in length, though in 1814, as the completion of the canal approached, a new packet was ordered specifically 62 feet long by 9 feet beam, so as to be capable of working through the short locks in Yorkshire. Jonathan Blundell & Sons were the operators from 1789 and the following year Henry Blundell also ran a market boat between Halsall and Liverpool twice a week. From 1805 the company again took back their operation, introducing new services over the next few years. From 1808 they operated daily to Wigan, with a market boat between Old Roan and Liverpool commencing in 1811. More trips were introduced on this service from 1813, providing a commuter service for the growing number of merchants living in Bootle and Litherland.

Brethertons provided the horses, being paid £900

Above: One of John Parkes' boats fitted with a grandstand for Aintree races. Good customers and their families, as well as employees, were invited for the day.

Right: The packet boat service as advertised in 1832.

LEEDS AND LIVERPOOL CANAL PACKETS
BETWEEN LIVERPOOL, WIGAN, AND MANCHESTER.

Summer Season.—On and after the 1st of May, a Packet-boat will leave Liverpool for Wigan and Manchester, every morning at six o'clock.

Another Packet also leaves Manchester for Wigan and Liverpool at a quarter-past six.

The Boat from Liverpool will arrive at Scarisbrick-bridge at a quarter-before eleven in the morning, at Wigan at a quarter-before three in the afternoon at Leigh at a quarter-past four, and at Manchester at a quarter-past eight in the evening.

The Boat from Manchester will arrive at Leigh at a quarter-past nine, Wigan at a quarter-before twelve in the morning, at Scarisbrick-bridge at four in the afternoon, and at Liverpool at half-past eight in the evening. Carriages attend the packets at Scarisbrick, to convey passengers to Southport, where they arrive at half-past eleven in the forenoon, and at five in the afternoon; thus providing a daily communication between the above places and Southport.

The extra Boat will leave Liverpool for Bootle, Linacre, and Crosby, every day at eight and ten in the morning, at half-past one and four in the afternoon, and at eight in the evening, except Sunday, on which day it leaves Liverpool at nine in the morning, at half-past one in the afternoon, and at seven in the evening.

Winter Season.—On and after the 1st of October, a Packet-boat leaves Liverpool for Wigan every morning at eight, another Packet-boat leaves Wigan for Liverpool every morning at eight, each arriving at their respective destinations, at five in the evening.

A Packet-boat leaves the Old Roan at seven in the morning, every day except Sunday, and arrives at Liverpool at nine in the morning.

The same Packet leaves Liverpool on return to the Old Roan at four in the evening.

A Packet-boat in the Winter Season from Manchester, every day at seven in the morning, arrives at Wigan at twelve at noon, and departs thence at two in the afternoon, on its return to Manchester, where it arrives at seven in the evening.

RATES AND FARES IN THE CANAL PACKETS.

FROM LIVERPOOL	Front.	Back
To Bank-hall Bridge and Bootle	0s 6d	0s 4
Orrell and Linacre	0 8	0 6
Litherland	0 8	0 6
Crosby	0 8	0 6
Ford	1 0	0 6
Aintree	1 3	0 10
Maghull	1 8	1 1
Scarisbrick	2 3	1 9
Burscough	3 0	2 0
Appley Bridge	3 6	2 6
Wigan	3 6	2 6
Leigh	5 6	3 6
Worsley	6 0	4 0
Manchester	6 0	4 0
From Bootle and Crosby to Manchester	6 0	4 0
Scarisbrick, ...do.	4 0	2 6
Wigan, ...do.	2 6	1 9
Leigh, ...do.	1 10	1 3
Astley, ...do.	1 8	1 0
Worsley, ...do.	1 4	0 8
Barton, ...do.	0 10	0 6

Intermediate distances in proportion.

---

annually, and there were stables at Maghull, Burscough and Wigan. In Liverpool a covered dock was built to protect the packets when they were not working, opposite Old Hall Street quay. It was from this quay that they operated, a bell being rung fifteen minutes before departure to ensure that everybody was aboard. Two horses pulled each boat, a rider on one blowing a horn to announce their coming and to urge on the horses. The packets continued to operate until the 1840s when railways quickly took their custom.

Pleasure Boats

There were always pleasure boats on the canal, though they were always subordinate to cargo boats. James Fletcher, the canal's Engineer, was asked in 1839 to take steps to prevent pleasure boats being used or let for hire on the canal on Sundays, which suggests that there were already locals regularly using the canal for leisure. As the nineteenth century progressed people had more spare time and by the 1890s there were several boathouses for pleasure craft erected near the residential area around Litherland. Several also moored near the bankranger's house in Maghull. The company charged a nominal sum for pleasure boats, though they were still subject to tolls if they passed through locks. The year 1932 saw the formation of the Mersey Motor Boat Club, who acquired canalside moorings at Litherland. With the post-war increase in leisure, they built a clubhouse adjacent to their new moorings at Lydiate, further moorings being provided

at Scarisbrick in the mid-1950s. Around this time, the Bootle Barge Company converted one of their boats into a trip boat called the *Bootle Belle*, for carrying groups on the canal. The Bootle Barge Company was owned by the Caddick family who had been involved with the canal for generations, and who went on the develop the *Water Witch* for cleaning rubbish out of the canal.

During the 1960s there was a concerted effort to close the canal, which was counteracted by the Inland Waterways Association. In 1965 they held their National Rally at Blackburn, and a smaller rally for the 72-foot-long narrow boats which could not pass through the shorter locks above Wigan was held by the Mersey Motor Boat Club at Lydiate. As part of this, boats sailed in convoy into Liverpool carrying local dignitaries, including Bessie Braddock. Three years later, the National Rally itself was held in Liverpool, and this had a major effect on opening up the potential of the canal to local planners. However, it was to be some thirty years before the full benefits began to be realised.

The Mersey Motor Boat Club's boatyard at Litherland in the 1950s.

By 1972, when a study group on the development of the canal reported, there were two rowing clubs near the Litherland tannery and the Sea Cadets had premises next to the boat club moorings. The report suggested that it was hoped to establish a floating youth club at Lightbody Street. One of the boats, which became available when the Wigan power station traffic ceased, was purchased and the author towed the boat into Liverpool. Unfortunately the project proved abortive, though in the 1980s a water sports centre was established in the old hydraulic pumping station at Athol Street. Other activity on the length over the last twenty-five years has been provided by the trip boat *Ambush* operated by Mike Sampson, while the local Inland Waterways Association members have an annual campaign cruise to Stanley Dock.

For many years, the canal's water supply often came from the heavily polluted River Douglas. There was little encouragement for recreational use and the poor quality of water deterred anglers. Access to the canal has traditionally been difficult, as a further

***TS Starling* in 1990, the Sea Cadets base in Litherland.**

discouragement. However, over the past two decades there have been considerable improvements. Openings onto the towpath have been provided in many places, and water from the Douglas is much cleaner. The resulting increase in fish numbers has begun to encourage anglers, while the cleaner water makes the towpath a more attractive place for a leisurely stroll.

6. THE TOWPATH TODAY

Much of the industry and warehousing which lined the canal has now disappeared together with the poorer quality housing, being replaced by modern developments. However, there is still much to see on a walk along the towpath from Aintree to Liverpool.

The canal crosses the valley of the River Alt at Aintree on a large embankment. On its Liverpool side there was a dredging tip where much of the mud removed from this section of the canal was dumped. The house built for Handcock, the bridge-keeper, was removed when this tip was formed. Around the corner can be seen Aintree Racecourse. Originally it was smaller, only occupying land on the Liverpool side of Melling Road Bridge, but was later enlarged. Before Old Roan Bridge, where the former Preston Turnpike crossed the canal, is an industrial site first suggest-

ed in the early 1920s for businesses which wanted to move out of the congested centre of Liverpool. Today, it is occupied by retail warehousing.

Past Old Roan we enter the 'remainder' stretch of waterway. Maintenance of this length is a lower priority than for the rest of the canal, and since the 1960s money for its maintenance has been restricted. At Netherton the canal winds its way through housing estates built during the Bootle slum clearances of the 1950s and '60s. Lunar Drive, Apollo Way and Aldrins Lane, the first roads encountered though the last to be built, are indicative of the time of their construction. For many years high fences made access to the towpath difficult, isolating the canal from use by the local community. This was typical of the canal in the Liverpool area, and improved access has been one of the major improvements in recent times. After passing through the housing estate we reach Gorsey Lane.

Boadicea and *Claymore*, two of H & R Ainscough's boats, high and dry at Aintree after the canal burst its banks in 1950.

A pipeline being installed under the canal in the mid-1950s during the construction of the first phase of the housing estate at Netherton.

Just before the bridge is the concrete edge of a wharf where many boats were loaded with imported goods during the Second World War. Cargoes were brought from the docks and stored here where bomb damage was less of a problem. It also saved time and danger

The fencing fitted to one of the swing bridges in Netherton is indicative of how planners viewed the canal, with no chance of legal use by locals.

The remains of the wartime wharf at Gorsey Lane.

for boat crews, who did not have to wait for cargoes in the docks.

After Gorsey Lane, the canal enters Rimrose Valley, which for many years was one of Liverpool's refuse tips, the land on the towpath side having been raised considerably as a result. A country park has been developed here, providing a much-needed open space for the local community. On the far side of the park is the Brookvale Local Nature Reserve. One thing to note on this section is the remains of swing bridges which once gave access to Rimrose Valley. At one time many of the bridges from here into Liverpool were

The tar distillery at Litherland has now been demolished.

Linacre Lane gasworks in 1977. Today little survives except for the towpath wall.

swing bridges. Today they have either been converted to road bridges or removed. Next to the new Fieldview footbridge were the remains of Litherland Tannery. They have recently been demolished, removing the last reminder of industrial use on the canalside before Litherland. Alongside the tannery site is a winding hole in the far canal bank which enabled boats delivering cargoes here to turn round. They are provided at many places along the canal, which was narrower than the sixty- or seventy-foot-long boats used on it. New housing faces the canal, unlike the earlier housing estates here, giving residents views across the country park to the docks. One feature to look for along the towpath is ramps out of the canal, sometimes covered with removable wooden planks,

which allowed boat horses which had fallen into the canal to be rescued, a not uncommon occurrence. Just before Litherland is the Sea Cadets' boathouse, TS Starling, a reminder that pleasure boating has long been a feature of this section of the canal. The *Mersey Motor Boat Club,* now based at Lydiate, was originally founded near here in the 1930s.

At Litherland the canal is crossed by the new bridge carrying traffic to and from the docks. Just beyond is the narrows where the lift bridge and its swinging predecessors were located. The bridge-keeper's house remains, as does the footbridge first provided in 1908, and the foundations of the lift bridge also survive. The tar distillery on the offside was one of the last survivors of the chemical industry, so long associated with the canal in Liverpool. But now it has closed, and the site is proposed for a new superstore, with a café overlooking the canal.

The next section of towpath now has little of interest, but after passing under the railway bridge carrying the branch from Bootle to Aintree there used to be several factories on the offside including a tannery built c.1890. Most have now been demolished to create a rather unsightly business park. Why not improve the canal frontage to provide a pleasant environment for workers here? Beyond Pennington Road Bridge were the remains of a lead works dating from around the turn of the century, with a tin smelters on the towpath side. This latter is now a small park. Linacre Gas Works is reached after Linacre Lane Bridge, the towpath wall revealing several bricked-up doorways where coal was delivered and gas tar removed by boat. Note also the remains of the railway bridge giving access to the works. Sports facilities are proposed for part of the gasworks site.

The gasworks wall continues along the towpath beyond Marsh Lane Bridge as far as Litherland Road. On the opposite bank was the Pine Grove destructor where Bootle's rubbish was dealt with, much of it being removed by boat for use as fertiliser on West Lancashire fields. Next door was Williams' Toffee Factory, with its chimney dating from 1911. This site is now proposed for housing. Litherland Road bridge, rebuilt in 1887, still has evidence of the vertical rollers used to stop boat hauling lines from wearing against the bridge structure. Such remains can be found on many of the bridges along the canal. Just through the bridge can be found a concrete stop place. Built during the Second World War, stop planks were inserted here at night so that if the canal was breached, as it was near Bank Hall, the amount of water lost would be restricted. Water was needed not just for boats, but also for fighting fires. In 1939, the Watch Committee proposed buying a fire boat for £600, part of the £9,000 spent on the Auxiliary Fire Service in Liverpool under the Air Raid Precautions Act.

At Stanley Road Bridge the towpath changes side. Canals are usually built on sloping ground, and the towpath was almost always on the 'lower' side, on top of the embankment built up to retain the canal water. Sometimes the towpath changed sides to help the boat horses which pulled boats. The strain on the towing line tended to pull the horse towards the canal, and changing sides gave the horses some respite. However, here the reason is to stop access from the towpath to the former canal company warehouse and arm at Carolina Street which were built around 1890. The towpath was changed then, again changing sides before the railway bridge near Oriel Road Station is reached. The warehouses have now been demolished, and new canalside housing built on the site. Short arms allowed boats to enter the warehouses, and the location of these can still be seen in the coping stones on the edge of the canal. The iron stump on the wharf is the remains of a crane used to unload boats.

After passing under the railway, Coffee House Bridge is next. Is the Wharf Inn a reminder of the Coffee House? Post-war industrial buildings now cover the site of Pugh's boatyard, and from here to Bank Hall the canal passes a variety of buildings, mainly housing as far as Millers Bridge on the towpath side, with the remains of industry on the offside. Amongst those on Canal Street, near Everton View footbridge, are Skinners Cooperage, which still manufactures wooden barrels, and the entrance to the former Dundee Sacking Works dated 1861. Next to Millers Bridge, a bus company occupies the former Jarvis Robinson Transport yard, which had stables along its Canal Street wall.

Warehousing appears beyond the bridge, though the mix of housing and commerce remains virtually to Bank Hall Bridge. On the offside, 250 yards before the bridge can be seen the Caledonia Foundry & Engine Works. The canal company's warehouse alongside the bridge dates from 1875. It straddled a short arm, but this has now been filled in and the entrance bricked up. There is also a covered wharf; the Leeds & Liverpool Canal Company often built wooden warehousing around 1900, where goods could be

One side of the wartime stop plank grooves at Bootle. At night planks were lowered into place and the canal was closed for traffic.

The warehouses at Bootle, seen here in 1978, have now been demolished and new housing built on the site.

Above & Right: Jarvis Robinson's yard next to Millers Bridge around 1925. Note the brick stables which ran along the back of the wharf.

transshipped in the dry. The open wharf became the base for John Parkes & Sons who converted an arm into a dry dock for their boats in the mid-1930s. The firm were the last to carry coal into Liverpool and were also involved in the manure traffic. Their fleet of boats was purchased by British Waterways shortly before the coal traffic ceased. On the towpath side of the canal opposite the wharf are a collection of warehouses and industrial buildings. In particular there is the former Hudsons Soap Works next to the bridge, another reminder of Liverpool's chemical industry. The buildings to the north of Bank Hall Bridge give the best impression of the former importance of the canal corridor to Liverpool's industrial base, though there has been some demolition in recent years.

Beyond Bank Hall Bridge, after passing the site of Canada Dock Goods Yard, we soon reach the railway bridge carrying the former Lancashire & Yorkshire Railway over the canal. Water to supply locomotives in their engine shed at Bankhall was taken from the canal just before this bridge. Coal was transshipped from railway to canal here, making deliveries to canalside works easier. Just through the bridge are the remains of a manure-loading wharf where the cast frames of the tips can be seen, though the rest of the wharf has been pleasantly landscaped, though unfortunately not down to the canalside. Tillotson's cardboard box factory was located behind this wharf, occupying the remaining space up to Sandhills Bridge

69

which was built in 1874. The entrance gateway and canalside foundations are all that remains. Opposite, against the towpath, are the oil and turpentine works of Banner & Co. where there are several blocked-up doorways onto the towpath, indicating the importance of the canal for transport.

After the bridge are the remains of the loading platform in front of Bee Mills, which was used for canal warehousing for many years. It eventually passed to the British American Tobacco Company Limited whose former works extend from here almost to Boundary Street. One building is currently being converted to flats. The towpath here overlooks the former site of Huskisson Goods Depot. The North Shore Mills, the site now the location for the Liverpool Film Studios, used to be next to Boundary Street Bridge, which shows clear evidence of strengthening and widening in the 1860s. It has two distinct arches, one of stone and the other of iron. Note the grooves caused by the ropes of boats being hauled along the canal. Bridges usually had rollers to avoid this, and the iron bearings of the roller supports can still be seen. There is also damage to the stonework, caused by bombing during the Second World War.

Around Boundary Street there has been considerable change, with new housing replacing the demolished industrial buildings. The hydraulic pumping station survived until the late 1990s following its conversion to a water sports centre, but it too has now been demolished. Alongside Leigh's Bridge on Athol Street is the Village Hall, with the Athol Vaults pub on Vauxhall Road being the last reminder of the days when most residents here lived in terraced housing. Between Athol Street and Lightbody Street was another gasworks site, but now no remains survive following the construction of housing. Under Lightbody Street bridge you can still find the bridge rollers which prevented damage from tow lines. The rollers are made from iron, though elsewhere on the canal they were usually wooden.

Just beyond the bridge, before the junction with the branch down to Stanley Dock, is one of the ramps which allowed boat horses to get out of the canal easily if they fell in. This happened when a boat jammed through hitting an obstruction, such as a moored boat, the tug on the tow line pulling the horse into the canal. Little of historical interest remains past the junction and the canal is now blocked at Burlington Street. This section remained in use until the 1960s, the concrete wharf opposite the branch dat-

The British American Tobacco factory has been undergoing conversion to housing for some years. The remains of Bee Mills can be seen in the foreground.

Bridge rollers, to protect stonework from wear by towing lines, were usually made from wood. On some more modern bridges they were made from iron, as here on Lightbody Street bridge. Grooves caused by the lack of rollers can be seen on many bridges along the canal.

An aerial view of the top of the Stanley Dock branch in 1984. The electrical junction compound in the centre was the start of the over-head power line which straddled the canal in Liverpool and Bootle. Most of the pylons were removed in 1991.

The canal beyond the dock branch had become very run down by 1987 when this photo was taken.

Today the end of the canal is in the Eldonian village. The success of this housing project has encouraged the construction of housing along much of this end of the canal.

ing from ten years earlier when it was hoped that the warehousing and carriage of tinned fruit would be developed there. Groceries were always one of the canal's main traffics, often delivered to Leeds, 127 miles away by canal as the milepost near the top of the locks shows.

In 1994 a new bridge replaced the old Gerard Bridge, and this provides access to the new Eldonian Housing Estate which has been built between the Stanley Locks and Chisenhale Street. The estate itself is something of historic interest as it shows the ability of a local community to survive and grow against the initial opposition of planners. The bridge in Chisenhale Street survives, as does the pub building alongside the bridge which was used by numerous boatmen and workers at Tate & Lyle's sugar refinery, though it is no longer a pub.

Parts of the canal's terminal basin and warehousing can still be found in Pall Mall. Note the brick wall at the northern end of the warehouses, which still has a door and window from the canal boatman's mission, part of the Mersey Mission to Seamen. The abutments of the railway bridge over the original canal basin, abandoned in the 1880s, can also be seen. The

importance of the canal can be noted in the name Leeds Street, and one of the canal's offices, used by the Wigan Coal & Iron Company, has been converted into a bar in Old Hall Street.

Most of the industrial buildings around the basin have been demolished, as has the housing. This area was bombed during the war – the canal company offices on Pall Mall were destroyed – and a memorial

The former Bridge Inn alongside the canal bridge in Chisenhale Street.

The locks down to Stanley Dock today provide a very different scene to that of the twentieth century. The industry and decay has been replaced by fashionable houses.

to those residents of Blackstock Gardens who died during an air raid in 1940 can be found on Vauxhall Road.

Returning to the section of canal still in use, across the entrance to the dock branch a pipeline now uses the footbridge supports which previously carried the towpath. The site of the lock cottage above the locks near this bridge can also be seen. Walking down the locks note the paddle gear. Until recently it was of an old pattern which had almost disappeared from the rest of the canal. New lock gates have removed some of this, but some of the ground paddles, those not on the gate, are of an older style. There are also the remains of hooks fixed in the ground at the head of some of the locks. In horse-boat days the tow-line was fastened to these, passing through a pulley on the boat's towing mast before leading to the horse. This halved the strain on the horse when pulling a boat out of the lock. The rope was eventually stopped from passing through the pulley by a peg in the line, which then slipped off the hook as the boat passed.

On the Lightbody Street side of the branch was the destructor operated by the Bootle Barge Company where they burnt rubbish removed from the docks, while below were several former wharfs originally built for the slate trade. Today, housing has replaced these, though the entrance to the Bridgewater Canal's basin, now filled in, is visible between the bottom lock and Great Howard Street Bridge. Opposite is the pump house, built in the 1930s to return water used by the locks back to the main canal. The discharge point at the top of the locks is on the south side of the branch. The wool warehouse, built by the Dock Board around the turn of the century, was located between the railway viaduct and Great Howard Street, an area which is now occupied by new housing.

Stanley Dock can only be reached by boat from the bottom of the locks, though there is now access for walkers onto Great Howard Street. No visit to the canal should ignore Hartley's warehouses which flanked the dock. Early in the twentieth century the tobacco warehouse was built, half of Stanley Dock being filled in to provide the site.

7. REDEVELOPMENT OF THE CANAL

Proposals for improving or reusing the canal date back to the early 1950s. Some were quite simple, such as the tractor designed for towing boats which was tried on the canal in 1954. It was too little too late, as the tonnages of cargo carried on the canal had been declining since the First World War. Coal shipments to Liverpool had reached over one million tons per year then, but now alternative fuels, such as electricity and oil, were more widely available. By the early 1960s, natural gas was being supplied from the North Sea, and traditional gasworks, such as those at Athol Street and Linacre Lane, were about to be phased out. The quality of the coal supplied by canalside collieries in Wigan was now less suitable for gas production, and the hard winter of

1963, when ice closed the canal for many weeks, was the final straw. Traffic on the Liverpool section of the canal ceased in 1964. There were attempts to develop new traffics in the 1970s, but these ultimately came to nothing.

The 1950s had seen new estates, part of Bootle's slum clearance programme, spring up on the canal's banks around Netherton, and the canal was to provide a fatal attraction to children. Some £12,500 was spent erecting six-feet-high fencing between Fleetwoods Bridge and the Taylor's Arms, but children still managed to reach the towpath. Some twenty drowned between 1951 and 1959. A vigilante patrol was suggested, but the main problem was that the towpath had become isolated, ac-

Catterick **passing Netherton towing a broken-down pleasure boat in the late 1950s, towards the end of regular traffic on the canal. In the background is one of the canal's steam tugs and some dredging pans.**

CANAL COULD BE LORRY
ROUTE FOR DOCKS TRAFFIC, SAYS M.P.

Turning A Dead Duck Into A Commercial Asset

LITTLE COST INVOLVED

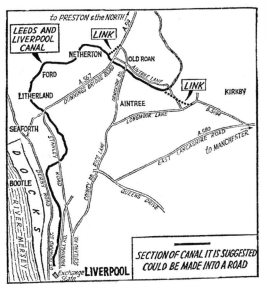

Alderman Simon Mahon, Labour M.P. for Bootle, advocates that the Leeds and Liverpool Canal, in the Merseyside area, should be turned into a lorry route.

He said last night that the change could be accomplished at comparatively little cost and with much less work than would be involved in the creation of a roadway from scratch. It would be of great value to the port of Liverpool.

The M.P. went on: "It requires no great feat of imagination to see that in this way a commercial and industrial dead duck could be transformed into one of the best assets we could have in the port."

The 1965 road scheme as reported in the Liverpool Echo.

cessible just by children, with adults kept out by the fencing. Planners had ignored the canal when designing the estates, rather than incorporating them into an overall scheme.

Elsewhere in Bootle, there were problems with children using the canal banks, even though the canal authorities, at the request of local authorities, had put locked gates on all the access points for many years. Not surprisingly, there were demands for the canal to be closed and filled in. One scheme, in 1965, suggested converting the canal into a road from Aintree to the docks. This was around the time that the canal terminus was filled in, and the new extension to Tate & Lyle's sugar refinery built over the route. In retrospect, this has proved one of the main factors in the canal's recent lack of use. To travel on a canal for leisure, there needs to be a destination which provides a safe and secure mooring, and possibly a boatyard or hire boat base. This is what the terminal basin in Pall Mall would have provided, near to the town centre and the many cultural attractions in Liverpool. Instead, the branch into the docks and the connection to the river was seen as the canal's terminus, though this provided none of the basics for leisure use. As a result, few pleasure boaters ever thought of visiting the city, especially with the reputation for vandalism acquired by the canal through Bootle.

Ever since nationalisation in 1948, it had been realised that the Leeds & Liverpool Canal was expensive to maintain and did not make a profit. In fact, it accounted for almost half of the national deficit. When Barbara Castle, the then Minister of Transport, came to review the national canal network in 1967, a good case was made for its closure, especially the Liverpool section. Instead she made the decision to designate the canal a cruising waterway, except for the section from Aintree into Liverpool which became a remainder waterway, where there were funds just for basic maintenance but none for improvement. It saved the canal, but resulted in a steady decline in amenity value. Over the years, there have been several projects to improve access and usage, but funding has always been a problem. As so often, there was money to identify the problem, but none to address it.

Members of the Mersey Motor Boat Club and the local branch of the Inland Waterways Association had long fought for recognition of the canal's potential on Merseyside. Then, in 1968, the Merseyside Civic Society published 'The Forgotten Way', the first academic study into ways of improving the environment along the canal. It identified the main areas which could be enhanced by the canal, and gave suggestions as to how this could be achieved. As a result, British Waterways and the local authorities set up a study group, which published 'The Leeds & Liverpool Canal: Retention and Improvement' in 1972. It looked in more depth at the problems, including accidents

Canal will be closed — but what follows?

The *Daily Post's* report on canal closure proposals.

The eight-mile stretch of canal from Old Roan bridge, Aintree, to Liverpool Docks—a stretch where twenty-six children have been drowned since 1955—is shortly to be closed to traffic by the British Waterways Board, but what will be done then has not been decided.

But no final decision has been taken on whether the shut-down will be for good and the canal filled in. The purpose of the closure is to enable an intensive study to be made of its future.

One of the things the study—to be carried out by the Board with the help of local authorities—will decide is whether it is feasible for the canal to be included in the Government's new inland waterways scheme announced yesterday by the Minister of Transport, Mrs Barbara Castle.

Speaking in London, yesterday, Mr Arnold Allen, general manager of the Board, said: " This is a canal which gives rise to very great problems. It is very little used at present."

"It seems they have decided it is of no ue, but they are still dithering," commented Mr Walter Alldritt, Labour M.P. for Liverpool's Scotland Division, last night.

And he threw out this challenge—"Are British Waterways frightened to make the recommendation that it should be filled in, or covered in, just in case they alone have to pay for the work to be done?"

Why wait any longer ?

Mr Alldritt, through whose constituency the canal passes, in the north end of Liverpool, said: " Why wait any longer to get rid of the problem this stretch of canal presents, in view of all that has been said and all the information already available? Surely, there is no justification for any more studying?"

He said he would be asking the Minister of Transport to make a positive statement about the future of this section of canal.

Mr Alldritt went on: " The Ministry need to give specific instructions to British Waterways about this stretch of canal," he said. "The Ministry, who have had enough representations and enouzh evidence to make up their minds, ought not to leave the question open indefinitely.

" If they do not feel, as it would appear they do not, that this stretch has any recreational potential, then they should say so and decide what is to be done with it."

and pollution, and came up with estimated costings for improvement. One of the main restraints on funding was the fact that the canal was still designated a 'remainder' waterway, and this has continued to have a detrimental effect over the years. However, canals were increasingly being seen as a positive feature for leisure and recreation, with Lancashire County Council producing a survey in 1972, and British Waterways publishing 'It Lends Itself Naturally' in 1973. Both concentrated on the sections of the canal away from Merseyside, where its 'cruising waterway' status encouraged investment.

Little was to happen to the Liverpool section of the canal regarding environmental improvements over the next fifteen years, the canal quietly declining and few people using its waters or banks. Then came the closure of Tate & Lyle's refinery and the development of the extremely successful Eldonian project. Housing designed by and for local people was built on the

The Mersey Motor Boat Club's boatyard at Litherland.

refinery site. In retrospect, it is a shame that the line of the canal was not preserved. The canal basin in Pall Mall is still recognisable behind the surviving canal warehouses, and had excellent development potential. Unfortunately, the benefits, both financial and environmental, of canalside improvement had not reached Liverpool then, and the new Eldonian housing estate was built without the possibility of reopening the canal. However, it did not turn its back on the surviving sections as might have happened. Instead, the canal forms an integral part of the estate, and is an attractive and increasingly safe place for boats to moor.

Sefton Borough Council was also encouraging use and improvement, together with British Waterways employing the first 'canal ranger' to actively promote

Today the canal basin is a car park, but warehouses still line the edge of the old canal, though the fronts which once were open for cargoes are now bricked up.

The Bootle warehouse site today. The arms into the warehouse can still be identified by the indentations in the canal bank between the two buildings.

The development of canalside housing, such as here at the top of the locks, was encouraged by the success of the Eldonian project.

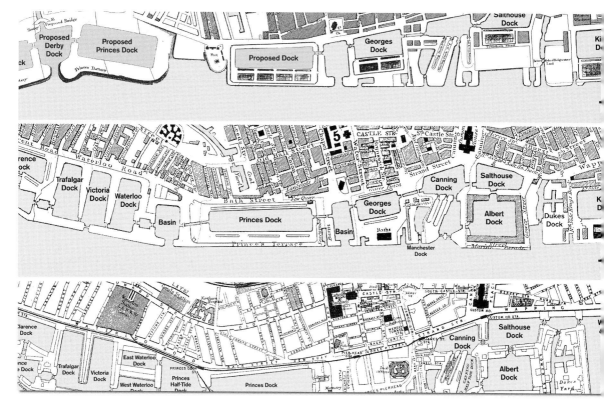

The water links, or lack of them, across Pier Head at different dates.

the canal in Bootle. Access points onto the towpath were created, and several schemes for canalside gardens with views onto the canal were carried through. Volunteers and schoolchildren have all been involved in environmental improvements. The early 1990s also saw the demolition of the overhead power lines, for so long an easy way of identifying the canal's route. It also saw the formation of the Merseyside Development Corporation which was to create a development strategy for the disused docks and the derelict industrial areas around the canal.

The New Canal to the South Docks

The 1990s had seen many disused canals restored, such as the Rochdale Canal and the Huddersfield Narrow Canal. By 2000, these schemes were well on the way to completion, overseen by the Waterways Regeneration Task Force, part of British Waterways, who had also just taken over management of the South Docks water space from English Partnerships. The Task Force, headed by Derek Cochrane, and local Waterway Manager Alan Bates, approached Liverpool City the Council's Liverpool City Vision with the sug-

gestion of rejoining the South Docks to the Leeds & Liverpool Canal by construction of a new waterway across Pier Head.

An outline scheme, with four different waterway routes between Princes Dock and Canning Dock, was drawn up and extensive public consultation undertaken in 2001. Overwhelming public support was given to the route across the Pier Head in front of the world renown Liver, Cunard and Dock Board buildings. The title, the Three Graces, seems to have been thought up for these buildings by some consultant looking at the redevelopment of Pier Head for one of the various regeneration groups operating in Liverpool at that time, much to the disgust of many Scousers.

Following the success of the public consultation, a project team was set up by British Waterways to look for funding and to liaise with the local authorities. Unlike other canal restoration schemes, here British Waterways owned no land and had no direct funding for the construction works. Feasibilty work was funded through the North West Development Agency (NWDA) and British Waterways Waterways Regenera-

A variety of flats and barges in the south docks. A large packing case is being transshipped from a Leeds & Liverpool Canal boat. It probably contains textile machinery which was an important return load from East Lancashire. Most traffic was from Liverpool or Leeds to destinations along the canal.

tion Task Force, and a detailed scheme was drawn up during 2003. The canal route had to be adjusted to fit into the 'Fourth Grace' scheme for a new building on Pier Head which was proposed in late-2003. The initial planning application was made in March 2004, and by August that year funding had been identified. The North West Development Agency would provide 50%, the rest coming from Europe through the European Regional Development Fund (ERDF) Objective 1 programme. British Waterways estimated cost for the canal was £17 million.

English Heritage objected to the new building as it would affect views of the existing buildings which were already listed. They required the new development to be more sympathetic. Following the objections to the new building, Liverpool Vision looked around for new developers to take on the site which resulted in changes to the planned route for the southern end of the new canal link. Architects EDAW were commissioned by the Council to look at the de-

George's Dock Passage into Canning Dock with a River Weaver steam and dumb barge, probably carrying salt. This was the route for boats from the Leeds & Liverpool Canal to the south docks before the construction of the Pier Head buildings.

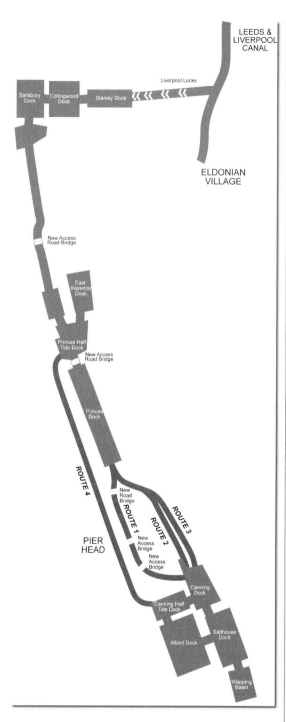

One of the views English Heritage were trying to retain. After crossing Pier Head, the canal will pass behind the Great Western Railway building before entering Canning Dock.

velopment of Pier Head as a whole, the canal scheme now having curved sections here, with stepped banks to create areas where people could sit in shelter from the wind and enjoy the canal side environmentlook at the canal. This was agreed by part of the Council, and a planning application was submitted in November 2004.

However, there were objections. Problems were caused partly by Liverpool's World Heritage Site application, and partly by some Council departments' desire for an open area. They objected, saying that the route and canal side terracing reduced the space available for events, and English Heritage were unhappy as views from the city centre along the streets between the Pier Head buildings would be interrupted.

The development of Mann Island, after the Fourth Grace proposal had been shelved, could not be final-

The original proposal, with the four lines suggested. Number one was alongside the Mersey, two was across Pier Head, three and four were behind the Liver building on the Goree, with four at high level with a lift at either end.

An artist's impression of the canal across Pier Head.

An aerial view of Pier Head c.1920. The tall chimney in the background is the Charter Street destructor, with the canal basin warehouses and office just to the left. In the foreground, Manchester Dock, with the GWR warehouse, is still in operation.

ised, and in December 2004 various options were suggested for the route here. Then, in February 2005, a new building for a Museum of Liverpool was proposed, requiring a further alteration to the canal. Its route now ran behind the old GWR building and across Museum land which required further extensive negotiations.

By March 2005, the route of the canal was virtually finalised, and a further planning application made. Across Pier Head the route had returned to a linear alignment ensuring the maximum area available for events. The two bridges over the canal had also been moved so that they aligned with the existing street network, preserving views between the various buildings. The proposed new tram route also had to be accommodated, with British Waterways objecting to the tram planning application in order to protect the construction of the new canal link. However, this was settled amicably before any legal action was taken.

April saw the NWDA, who owned Mann Island, nominate their preferred developer for this site, a joint venture between Neptune Developments and Countryside Properties. The buildings they proposed had to undergo adjustment so that their height and shape did not interfere with views of the existing Pier Head buildings. An outline plan for a mixed use development was drawn up in July 2005. This had required various route alterations to the canal relative

The remains of Manchester Dock have been unearthed during redevelopment of the museum site. The GWR warehouse can be seen behind and to the right of the lock gates.

81

The tunnel under the cruise liner terminal under construction early in 2007

to the new buildings, creating a better use of space and more open space for the canal. The alterations here required a slight enlarging of the southern canal water space on Pier Head so that longer boats could negotiate the corner more easily.

With all the partners at Pier Head now fully behind the canal, and the design for the route finalised, a new planning application to take account of the finalised design at Mann Island was submitted in August 2005. Permission was granted early in 2006, allowing detailed design work to go ahead.

Planning the route across Pier Head was the most difficult section of the new canal as there were several land owners — Peel Holdings, Liverpool City Council, National Museums & Galleries in Liverpool, and North West Development Agency — whose agreement had to be obtained. The canal had to fit in with other developments on the site, and with such complex negotiations, it is small wonder that planning took so long. British Waterways could have applied for an Act of Parliament for the canal which would

have given them ownership of the land. However, this was thought to be too complicated and time-consuming, and agreement with land owners for the lease of the required land was undertaken instead.

The more northerly section of the route through the old docks was not so difficult to arrange. Initially the Central Dock area was owned by the Mersey Docks & Harbour Company, but more recently these docks have been purchased by Peel Holdings resulting in two sets of negotiation. Both have hinged on the benefit to developers of waterside areas, something which is well established but difficult for land owners to admit during negotiation.

Trafalgar and Clarence Docks have both been infilled, but creating a new water channel will not be difficult as one of the old dock walls can be used to create one canal bank. West Waterloo Dock was also earmarked for infill, but here the water space will now be retained, to leave wide open water to the end of Princes Dock where the new channel across Pier Head begins.

Above: Work underway excavating the new canal across Pier Head in April 2007.

Below: Canal Boats in Salthouse Dock for the Mersey River Festival.

The first section of the new canal, close to Princes Dock, crosses what the developer considers to be the most valuable plot of land in Liverpool, so to maximise the space, the canal route is located adjacent to the eastern boundary of the plot, as far to the east as possible. The adjacent new cruise liner terminal is already under construction, and the section of canal straddling the old floating roadway basin had to be constructed before the funding for the full project was confirmed. Delay here would have caused major disruption to the various developments around Pier Head and cost much more than construction as part of the cruise liner terminal project. To overcome this the canal tunnel here has been financed by the NWDA, costing half a million pounds, but without any financial repercussions resulting from the possibility of the rest of the canal not being completed. Without this gesture, it is unlikely that the canal could be completed for 2008.

Elsewhere on the route there will have to be improvements. The locks down to Stanley Dock are being refurbished, and the old water pumping system reinstated to ensure that there is sufficient water for

boats using them. Because the canal is now isolated from the operational North Docks, it is probable that Salisbury Dock Barge Dock will have to be reinstated to create a simple route from the canal into the Mersey. However, this is not part of the current scheme as there are engineering problems in restoring such deep old locks, but it must certainly form part of any project to redevelop Stanley and Collingwood Docks. It will possibly be included in the development of a marina, which would be a major attraction and encourage greater use of the canal.

Appendices

CHRONOLOGY OF THE LEEDS & LIVERPOOL CANAL

1712	Navigations proposed for the River Douglas, to Wigan, and the Mersey and Irwell, to Manchester.
1713	River Douglas Navigation Bill rejected by Parliament.
1720	River Douglas Navigation Act passed, Thomas Steers and William Squire named as undertakers.
1731	Alexander Leigh and Alexander Radcliffe take over as undertakers for the Douglas Navigation.
1736	Mersey & Irwell Navigation opened.
1737	Robert Holt replaces Alexander Radcliffe as undertaker.
1738	Work starts on building the Douglas Navigation.
1742	Douglas Navigation opened.
1757	Sankey Brook Navigation opened.
1765	Bridgewater Canal opened to Manchester.
	Canal from Leeds to Preston proposed by John Stanhope and surveyed by John Longbotham.
1766	Public meeting at Bradford to discuss the scheme and subscription opened to pay for detailed plans.
1767	Proposed canal now to run from Leeds to Liverpool.
1768	First meeting in Lancashire about the canal.
1769	Liverpool promoters suggest that the canal should pass through Burnley and Blackburn, instead of through Whalley as proposed by Longbotham.
1770	First Leeds & Liverpool Canal Act passed, authorising a line via Skipton, Gargrave, Colne, Whalley, Walton-le-Dale and Parbold.
1772	Alexander Leigh's shares in the Douglas Navigation purchased.
	Liverpool Canal Bill, proposing to link Liverpool with Wigan, fails to obtain Parliamentary assent.
1773	Leeds & Liverpool Canal opened from Bingley to Skipton.
1774	Leeds & Liverpool Canal opened from Liverpool to Gathurst, and then by Douglas Navigation to Wigan. The sections from Skipton to Gargrave, and Bradford to Shipley and Bingley also opened.
	Leeds & Selby Canal Bill, and the Settle Canal Bill, fail to obtain Parliamentary assent.
1777	Leeds & Liverpool Canal opened from Shipley to Leeds.
	Work on constructing the main line to cease, all available capital having been spent.

CHRONOLOGY OF THE LEEDS & LIVERPOOL CANAL (Cont'd)

1780   Leeds & Liverpool Canal opened from Gathurst to Wigan.

1781   Douglas Navigation closed following the opening of the branch canal from Burscough to Rufford and Sollom Lock.

1783   Second Leeds & Liverpool Canal Act passed, allowing the River Douglas Navigation to be purchased.

1790   Third Leeds & Liverpool Canal Act passed, authorising the line to be altered to avoid the aqueduct at Whalley Nab.

1791   Building of the canal recommences westward from Gargrave.

1792   Lancaster Canal Act passed.

1793   Bill for a deviation of the line through Burnley, Blackburn and Chorley, to the canal at Wigan, fails to obtain Parliamentary assent.

1794   Fourth Leeds & Liverpool Canal Act passed, authorising the deviation through East Lancashire.

1796   Leeds & Liverpool Canal opened to Burnley following the completion of Foulridge Tunnel.

1799   Southern section of the Lancaster Canal opened from Haigh to Wheelton.

1801   Leeds & Liverpool Canal opened from Burnley to Henfield.

        Duke of Bridgewater agrees to Leigh Branch.

1805   As a result of the Croston Drainage Scheme, the Rufford Branch is extended from Sollom Lock to Tarleton.

1809   Bill for Leigh Branch fails in Parliament.

1810   Leeds & Liverpool Canal opened from Henfield to Blackburn.

        The use of the Lancaster Canal between Heapey and Haigh agreed.

1816   Leeds & Liverpool Canal completed and opened throughout.

1819   Fifth Leeds & Liverpool Canal Act passed, authorising the construction of the Leigh Branch.

1820   Leigh Branch opened.

1826   Liverpool & Manchester Railway Act passed.

1846   Liverpool Dock Branch opened after construction by Jesse Hartley, Liverpool's Dock Engineer.

1848   Leeds & Liverpool Canal Company takes over the carriage of merchandise.

1850   Merchandise traffic leased to railway consortium.

        Head office moved to Liverpool.

1864   Southern section of the Lancaster Canal leased by the Leeds & Liverpool Canal.

CHRONOLOGY OF THE LEEDS & LIVERPOOL CANAL (Cont'd)

1874   Leeds & Liverpool Canal Company resume operation of merchandise traffic following the termination of the railway lease.

1882   Basin at Liverpool reconstructed.

1891   Sixth Leeds & Liverpool Canal Act, authorising construction of Winterburn Reservoir.

1892   Seventh Leeds & Liverpool Canal Act, altering the rating of the canal.

1893   Leeds & Liverpool Canal, Rates, Tolls, and Charges Order introduced by Parliament.

1905   Eighth Leeds & Liverpool Canal Act, extending the time allowed for the construction of further reservoirs.

1921   Canal Company disposes of its carrying fleet.

1928   Ninth Leeds & Liverpool Canal Act, altering the tolls charged.

1948   Following nationalisation, canal controlled by the Docks & Inland Waterways Executive.

1953   British Transport Waterways set up and take over responsibility for the canal.

1960   Regular traffic over the summit level ceases.

1963   British Waterways Board formed.

1964   The last traffic on the main line finishes.

1972   Regular trade on the canal ceases when the coal traffic to Wigan Power Station stops.

        First study into improving the canal in Liverpool.

1980s   Some carrying continued by enthusiasts, with regular shipments of grain between Liverpool and Manchester for around one year.

c.1990 Eldonian project begun.

2000   Canal across Pier Head linking the Central and South Docks proposed.

2008   Canal link opened?

BRIDGES: LIVERPOOL TO OLD ROAN

In 1775, there were 19 bridges between the terminal basin and Old Road, and only one was a stone arch bridge, all the rest being swing bridges. These held up traffic, both on the canal and on the road, and they were soon being replaced. In 1784, Sandhills Bridge was converted, in 1787 Old Roan Bridge, and then in 1790 Stamp House Bridge.

The 1790 Act for the canal, its third Act, included a clause which required the company to replace swing bridges with stone bridges where possible, and the following year it was proposed to convert four bridges annually, starting with Lydiate, Down Holland and Coffee House Bridges. In 1799 it was decided to round off edges on the stone bridges in Lancashire to protect them from tow lines which were rubbing on the corners. Perhaps it was at this time that the bridge rollers, typical of the Leeds & Liverpool, were introduced.

Bridges from Liverpool Basin to Old Roan

Those numbered on the left were listed in 1775. The names on the right are for the bridges added since then, and give any change in name over time.

			Chisenhale Street Bridge	1802
			Burlington Street Bridge	c.1850
			(Tekary St.) Gerrards Br.	1827 (removed 1898)
			Lightbody Street Bridge	1840s (with locks?)
			Leigh Bridge	1791 Athol Street
			Boundary Street Bridge	1860s?
1	Moss's Bridge	Kirkdale	Sandhills Bridge	
2	Bank Hall Bridge	Bootle	Bank Bridge	
3	Middle Marsh Bridge	Bootle	Marsh Bridge, Sandy Lane, Balliol Road	
4	Bootle Mill Bridge	Bootle	Coffee House Bridge	
			Stanley Road Bridge	?
5	Bootle Town Bridge	Bootle	Stamp House Bridge	Litherland Road Bridge
			Marsh Lane Bridge	?
6	Linecar Bridge	Linecar	Linacre Road Bridge	
7	Litherland Road Bridge	Litherland	Litherland Lift Bridge	Red Lion Bridge
8	Whitehead's Bridge	Litherland	Litherland Little Bridge	Shepherd's Bridge
9	Quarry Bridge	Litherland	(removed)	
10	Ford or Darran's Bridge	Litherland	Ford Bridge	Brown's Bridge
11	Rushton's Bridge	Ford	Webster Bridge	
12	Gausey Lane Bridge	Ford	Gorsey Lane Bridge	
13	Buckley Hill Br. (arch)	Sefton		
14	Buckley Hill 2nd arch br.	Sefton	Fleetwood Lane Bridge	Rollinson's Bridge
15	Harrop's Barn Bridge	Sefton	Heart's Barn (removed)	
16	Netherton Green Bridge	Sefton	Netherton Bridge	
17	Old Bootle's Bridge	Sefton	Copy Bridge	
18	Stand Park Bridge	Sefton	Stand Bridge	
19	Old Roan Bridge	Aintree		

1768 Liverpool Committee

At a meeting held at the Golden Lyon in Liverpoole on the 9th day of December 1768, agreeable to advertisements in the Publick Papers.

Resolved that a proper number of Gentlemen shall be appointed to meet the Gentlemen of Yorkshire on Monday the 19th day of December instant at Burnley in this County to consider of proper measures to carry the above mentioned plan into execution.

Jno. Wyke	Watch Maker	Dale Street
Will. Davenport	Merchant	Drury Lane
Jno. Brownell	Attorney	Water Street
Robt. Richmond	Attorney	Chapel Street
Hen. Rathmell		
Ralph Earl	Timber Merchant	School Lane
John Parr	Merchant	Wolstenholmes Square
Tho. Smyth	Old Hall Street	
Wm. James	Merchant	Rainfords Buildings
Anth. Whyte	Merchant	Duke Street
Tho Wyckliffe	Merchant	Duke Street
Clayton Care	Merchant	Water Street
H. Lake	Attorney	Water Street
Thomas Ryan	Merchant	Chapel Street
Alex. Nottingham	Merchant	Fenwicks Alley
Thomas Earle	Merchant	King Street
Jonas Bold		
Thos.Whittaker	Merchant	Park Lane
Will. Crosbie Junr.	Merchant	Pool Lane
Wm. Rathbone		
John Sparling	Merchant	Duke Street
Mat. Stronge (Mayor)	Corporation Treasurer	Paradise Street
John Tarleton	Castle Street	
Thomas Case (Alderman)	Merchant	Water Street
James Hollinshead (Alderman)	Gentleman	Harrington Street
John Walker	Merchant	Frog Lane
J. Colquitt	Customs Collector	Hanover Street
J. MacKay	Joiner	Hanover Street
Thos. Fazackerley		
Peers Leigh		
Jon. Blundell	Merchant	Water Street
Jos. Taylor		
John Williamson (Alderman)	Beer Brewer	Lancelot Hey
Benj. Heywood	Merchant	Hanover Street
Jon. Brooks	Merchant	Old Hall Street
Jno. Yate	Corn Dealer	Bootle Mills
Thos. Falkner	Merchant	Old Hall Street

Canal Company Minutes PRO 846/1

A letter from a canal worker to the L&LC committee after looking at the Sankey Navigation's coal trade

Wigan Sept 14th 1816

Statement of the Tuneg watter and other nesessary thigs on the Sankey Canall Clarks Colliery and rodes Mr. Blundel and Mr. Hustlers Collereys in Winstanley Orell and setrey.

Mr Woods acount he has 3 sloops on the Sankey trades to Nant Wich Coles at and near Sant Ellen is put on board at 8/4 per Tun 24 Hundred to the tun Canell Do put on bord 12s per Tun of 24 Hundred Canall Dues 1s per tun of 24 Hundred Frite 3s per tun to Liverpool and som 3s 4d by some vesels the state of the watter by the Locktentr and Carpenter Repairin a Brige near the nue dubell rise or Ingan Lock They informed me thay are never short of watter onley in verey dry Seasons but has not so much trade as formerley owin to the Salt Works not doin much at Nant Wich thay had pased throu the ferry Lock from 30 to 50 Bots in one day formerley but Could do more then thay do now but the Coale trade is verey slack at present hadack Lock pear head Coals Curnall Lees Capten informed me Cols 8s 4d per tun 24 hundred at Stock and Eckels Colery 8s 4d at the Union Colierey 8s 4d Canell 12s all 24 hundred to the Tun the Ingan Lifts the water into Sant Ellen Lock out of Lower pound in to the hier poand Clark Coles ar put on board at Black brook thhe man informed me thay sould to the Contrey at $5\frac{1}{2}$ per hundred but did not know what thay was to the Canall.

Mr Clark Coals Costs Cartin 3s per tun of 20 Hudred to the tun Mr. Daglas makes the Carters have carts to hould 2 tun with in the sides thay bring 2 ton at once and gose twis Some days and once others but will not goo above once in winter severall of the Carters tould me it was a verey bad job thay have the Bars Cleared besides th 3s but som of the Carters says thay had as good play as Cart Coals at that price the Distans from the first pit from the Wharf at Black Brook it will be I think 6 miles some say $5\frac{1}{2}$ miles and some say 6 and some more thay go $3\frac{1}{2}$ miles in narow Lanes Not good rod mow thay obliged to have 3 horse from the pit at top of the hill and the rode fals for above a mile befor we com near whear thay are sinkin for Mr Blundell the nearest of Blundels pits to the Sankey is 7 or $7\frac{1}{2}$ miles and 2 mils all up the hill to the top of winstanley thos cols would Cost 6s per tun Cartin to Sankey Canall if noot more And thay have a good Iron raleway down to the Leeds and Liverpool Canall not above $2\frac{1}{2}$ miles and som of the pits Not above 1 mile or a mile and a half Mr Clarks whear thay are Cartin to Sankey is not $3\frac{1}{2}$ miles to the Liverpol Canall down a good raleway the rale way Lade in the Rode Side for 5 or 6 pits a regerall desent down touards the Crook Mr Hustlers is still forder of the Sankey Mr Clarks Canot Cart to Sankey onley 2 or 3 pits and that will be found a verey great Exspence The Woman at turnpike Gate sade 2 or 3 or 4 Carts per day Somtims 10 thear was 7 on Friday over.

The Woman at the Bare says the Carters do not think of doin much after the water is on the Wigen Canall. The Sankey Canall is soplide part of th Brock and part by Reservoies the peopell in the Cuntrey thinks Daglas verey folish to Cart Cols 3 or 4 Mile furder then he neds down a bad rode and has A good rale way to take them down but he has Informed maney peopell that I talked with that the Coles will Cost 2s per tun Les by the Sankey then thay will by the Leeds and Liverpool Canall but you will know about that youer self this I hope will be what you wanted and give Sattis faction I did not se one person that knowed me all the day nor aksed my name but one

Dear Sir I Reman your Friend Sinsearley
Thos Clapham

BIBLIOGRAPHY

Clarke, Mike, *The Leeds & Liverpool Canal; a history and guide*, Lancaster: Carnegie, 1990, ISBN 0 948789 40 9.

Clarke, Mike & Hewitt, Allison, *Liverpool and its Canal*, Liverpool: Merseyside Port Folios, 1992, ISBN 0 9516129 3 X (1st edition).

Clarke, Mike, 'Thomas Steers', in Dock *Engineers and Dock Engineering: papers presented at a research day school*, Merseyside Maritime Museum, 13 February 1993.

Hadfield, Charles and Biddle, Gordon, *The canals of North West England*, 2 vols, Newton Abbot: David & Charles, 1970.

Harris, J R, 'Early Liverpool Canal Controversies', in *Liverpool & Merseyside, Essays in the economic and social history of the port and its hinterland*, London: Cass, 1969, ISBN 0 7146 1314 2.

Hartley, John, *Seets in Yorkshire and Lancashire* (c.1900)

Killick, H. F., 'Notes on the early history of the Leeds and Liverpool Canal', *Bradford Antiquary* n.s.vol.2, July 1897.

Paget-Tomlinson, Edward, *Illustrated History of Canal and River Navigations*, Sheffield: Sheffield Academic Press, 1993; new ed. Ashbourne, Landmark Publishing, 2006.

Rosbottom, Ernest, *Burscough: the story of an agricultural village*, Lancaster: Carnegie, 1987.

Wheat, Geoff, *Leeds and Liverpool canal craft*, Swinton: Northern Counties Carriers, 1972.

Wheat, Geoff, *Canal Transport Limited*, Reading: Maiwand, 1999.

Index